CHRIST EMPOWERED LIVING

Reflecting God's Design

LifeWay Press
Nashville, Tennessee

ISBN 0-6330-9153-7

This book is course CG-0840 in the category Personal Life
of the Christian Growth Study Plan.

Dewey Decimal Classification Number: 248.84
Subject Headings: CHRISTIAN LIFE \ SIN \ SALVATION

Cover photographed by Jon Rodda at Waverly Abbey House, Farnham, England.

To order additional copies of this resource, write to LifeWay Church Resources
Customer Service; One LifeWay Plaza; Nashville, TN 37234-0013;
fax (615) 251-5933; phone toll free (800) 458-2772;
email *customerservice@lifeway.com;* order online at *www.lifeway.com;*
or visit the LifeWay Christian Store serving you.

Printed in the United States of America

Leadership and Adult Publishing
LifeWay Church Resources
One LifeWay Plaza
Nashville, TN 37234-0175

Contents

Meet the Presenter 4

How to Use This Resource .5

WEEK 1 ✦ Meet Your Designer 6

WEEK 2 ✦ How it All Went Wrong 20

WEEK 3 ✦ The Effects of the Fall 34

WEEK 4 ✦ Depravity: Deeper Than You Think 48

WEEK 5 ✦ Restoring the Image 62

WEEK 6 ✦ The Dynamic for Change 76

WEEK 7 ✦ Making the Restoration Complete 90

WEEK 8 ✦ A Final Perspective 104

Knowing God Personally .116

Leader Guide 118

Attendance Form 126

Christian Growth Study Plan 127

MEET THE PRESENTER

Selwyn Hughes is best known for his series of bimonthly themed devotional studies, *Every Day with Jesus,* read by nearly a half a million believers around the world each day.

Whether in Great Britain or Africa, China or Europe, Selwyn's message is victorious Christian living. The Welsh-born evangelist is the founder of Crusade for World Revival, located at Waverley Abby House in Farnham, England, near London. Founded in 1965, CWR is a training and publishing ministry.

Selwyn is the author of the best-selling books, *Every Day Light* and *Water for the Soul.*

"Selwyn Hughes leads you and me to the light of Scripture with extraordinary skill and inspiration. Instead of representing light with paint and brushes and canvas, his tools are Bible passages, prayer, and rich insightful commentary."—Thomas Kinkade

"Selwyn is a sure and wise guide to all who ... realize they are on a journey, a sometimes difficult one, to God. It is a joy to commend this book to a worldwide audience." —Dr. Larry Crabb

BETTY HASSLER wrote the personal learning activities and the Leader Guide. Betty has contributed to many LifeWay Press publications, including *Basics for Baptists, What Every Mom Needs, Transformed Lives,* and numerous other magazine and teacher training material. Betty is Instructional and Biblical Specialist, Leadership and Adult Publishing, at LifeWay Church Resources. She and her pastor husband live in Antioch, Tennessee.

How to Use This Resource

Welcome to *Christ Empowered Living: Reflecting God's Design*. Over the next eight weeks you will follow the biblical story from creation and the fall to Christ as the only answer to restoring what God had in mind when He made us.

Your presenter, Selwyn Hughes, will share his unique interpretations and insights to problems we face on a daily basis. Here are a few examples.

- Why do I lack willpower to conquer besetting sins?
- If Christ is in me, why do I experience defeat in trying to lead a Christian life?
- What does God really expect of me in this earthly body?

Rev. Hughes will provide these answers and more each week in a 20-25 minute DVD session.

Session 1

In session 1, you will be given this printed resource, complete with a viewer guide at the beginning of week 1. You will be asked to fill in the spaces as Rev. Hughes delivers his message. Then your group will share the answers and briefly discuss what you heard. Bring your Bible to class.

During the Week

During the week following each session, you will complete a reading assignment which will provide further information and a review of each session's video presentation.

This interactive study can be read in one sitting or it can be read over five days. You will benefit from reading from major heading to major heading over several days. You will retain more information.

You will note several types of personal learning activities which are designed to help you internalize the life-changing message of this resource. Please don't bypass these activities and deprive yourself of an opportunity to grow.

Set aside a certain time and place five times a week to study each week's content. If you read from major heading to the next major heading, you will take less than 20 minutes to process the information and complete personal learning activities.

During the Sessions

Christ Empowered Living is intended to be discussed in a weekly group meeting, which will offer you the insights of others who are on a similar spiritual journey.

The first half of each session the facilitator will lead participants to discuss the previous week's reading assignment. You will have an opportunity to ask questions and make observations.

During the second half of each session, you will watch the next video and complete the viewer guide. The facilitator will ask someone to review their answers in the guide so that everyone will be assurred of a correct response.

Each week's reading assignment will be the same. In some studies members read the material first and then see a video. In this study, you will read the material that supplements the video you have seen in class.

Session 8

During the first 15 minutes of the class you will discuss the reading material in week 7. Next will be the video presentation, followed by a discussion of the viewer guide. Together, you, your facilitator, and other participants will walk through the supplementary material for week 8 in the last 15 minutes of class.

You are encouraged to read week 8 after session 8 on your own. Or, members can choose to meet a final time to review this material.

Session 1: Meet Your Designer

One thing that makes Christianity different from every other religion is that its founder who was crucified and lay in a grave for three days came back from the dead to live His life in and through His followers.

1. Christ _____, _____, and _____ in us.

   If Christ lives in the lives of His followers, why do so many of His disciples feel

   overcome by such things as fear, guilt, irritation, frustration, anger, and so on?

2. In attempting to understand the roots of human problems and behavior, a basic

   principle must be understood: All _____ is caused, and

   the causes are multiple.

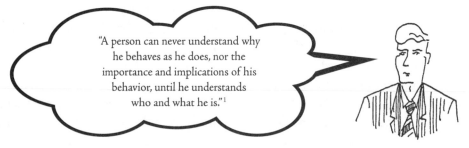

"A person can never understand why he behaves as he does, nor the importance and implications of his behavior, until he understands who and what he is."[1]

3. Only as we understand the thrilling design that has gone into the construction

   of our _____ can we understand why we do what we do.

4. Who and what are we? We are beings made in the _____ of God.

   God paid us the highest compliment He could when He made us in His Image.

God is a personal being who _____.
The first thing said about God in Scripture is that He is a relational being. "In the beginning God [*Elohim:* plural] created the heavens and the earth" (Gen. 1:1).

5. God is one yet three persons: _____, _____, _____.

6. Before sin entered the garden, Adam and Eve related to one another on earth

as the _____ relates to one another in heaven.

God is a rational being who _____.

7. Adam reflected his God-given ability to think by naming the _____.

"He [God] brought them to the man to see what he would name them" (Gen. 2:19).

8. Adam reflected his God-given ability to think by naming the _____.

" 'She shall be called "woman," for she was taken out of man' " (Gen. 2:23).

God is an emotional being who _____.

9. Scripture abounds with _____ imagery.

10. Adam demonstrated _____ when he first encountered his wife (Gen. 2:23).

11. God _____ and He has designed His human creation to _____ also.

God is a volitional being who _____.

12. God created the world by an act of His _____ (Gen. 1; Rev. 4:11).

13. Ruling over creation implies _____.

14. Adam and Eve were created in God's image:

Like God, they could _____.Like God, they could _____.

Like God, they could _____. Like God, they could _____.

MEET YOUR DESIGNER

❖

"From one man he made every nation of men, that they should
inhabit the whole earth; and he determined the times set
for them and the exact places where they should live."

ACTS 17:26

On July 23, 1969, Edwin R. Aldrin ("Buzz" to his family and friends) was
returning to earth on the *Apollo 11* spacecraft from having set foot on the
moon. In a broadcast he made during that historic flight, he read:

> When I consider your heavens,
>   the work of your fingers,
> the moon and the stars,
>   which you have set in place,
> what is man that you are mindful of him,
>   the son of man that you care for him? (Ps. 8:3-4).

No doubt that question will be asked as long as the human race continues.
" 'What is man that you make so much of him, that you give him so much
attention?' " (Job 7:17). What is man? Some seek to magnify man, to elevate
him to a position higher than Scripture accords him, but others look to
detract from his scriptural importance and place in the universe. I came
across this in a science textbook in my library: "Man is a cosmic accident,
a bubble which has blown up on the surface of some oozy primordial
swamp and is designed to burst into oblivion."

Today's evolutionary-oriented climate popularly sees human beings as
nothing more than superior animals. Many say that the origin of life is a
mystery. Not so. Someone can speak authoritatively about the origin of
man, and that someone is the One who originated the species—the Creator
himself. This week we will consider from the pages of the Bible, what the
Almighty says about human origin.

As you read, look for the answers to these key questions:
1. What does it mean to say we are made in the image of God?
2. What do we need to learn about God to better understand ourselves?
3. In what ways were the first human pair like God?

E. Stanley Jones tells the story of a little boy who one Christmas day stood for several minutes before a picture of his absent father and then turned to his mother and said wistfully: "How I wish father would step out of the picture." One day our Father stepped out of the picture at Bethlehem. John's Gospel says simply but sublimely: "The Word became flesh and made his dwelling among us" (John 1:14).

This exciting truth, one of the clearest themes running through the New Testament, is that once we commit our lives to Jesus Christ, He actually comes to live His life in us and through us. We have the life of Christ as our life. Not just outside of us, but inside us. Christ actually thinks and wills and feels in us. That's the promise held out to all who make Jesus Christ Lord of their lives.

Now if it is true that Christ lives in us, why are we so often overcome by such things as fear, anxiety, guilt, irritation, frustration, and so on? On one occasion a well-known keynote speaker on the Christian women's conference circuit put this question to me: why is it when I pick up a sharp knife in my kitchen, I feel strangely compelled to cut myself with it?

A man told me whenever he entered a store with a large number of entrances and exits, he would be seized with panic. The thought that he might return to the street through any other door than the one he entered set up such tremendous anxiety that sometimes he required medical assistance.

Often these feelings are so crippling and debilitating that they seem to overpower the life of Christ within us and cause us to behave in ways that are contrary to the spirit of Jesus Christ. Why is that so?

Do you identify with this question? To what degree do you feel Christ controls your behavior? Place an X on the line.

|—————————————————|—————————————————|

Little Control   Some Control   Christ Controlled

"I have been crucified with Christ and I no longer live, but Christ lives in me. The life I live in the body, I live by faith in the Son of God, who loved me and gave himself for me."

—Galatians 2:20

We will examine this issue together in this study, but let me lay down a basic presupposition which I think will be accepted by everyone: All behavior is caused, and the causes are multiple.

In other words, the reasons why we behave the way we do can be traced back to a number of causes. We sometimes look at people who behave in ways that we find difficult to understand, and we wonder why does he do that? Or why does she behave in that way? Christians can behave strangely, as can non-Christians.

Theories about human motivation and what makes people tick quickly get translated into counseling models. Solutions range from taking medication, physical exercise, reparenting, casting out demons, changing self-talk, getting needs met, avoiding decision-making when your stars are not properly aligned to getting in touch with inner pain and other popular advice.

All behavior is caused, and the causes are multiple.

Have you tried any of these self-help models? ❏ Yes ❏ No

If so, which ones? _____

What was the outcome? _____

I believe God has something to say about what lies behind human behavior. When we want the real truth about why we do the things we do, He is the Consultant par excellence. Read the statement of a Christian psychiatrist by the name of James Mallory in his book, *The Kink and I:* "A person can never understand why he behaves as he does, nor the importance and implications of his behavior, until he understands who and what he is."[2]

If it is true, as James Mallory says, that we can never understand why we behave the way we do until we understand who and what we are, then the question arises: who and what are we?

In other words, it is not until we understand something of the thrilling design that has gone into the construction of our being and how that design has been violated that we can figure out why we do what we do. I have made a special study of psychology, but I know of no book or course that gets to the real reasons like Scripture. God made us to function in a certain way, and unless we understand that design, we will not function in the way we ought to.

How do we begin to get a handle on this issue? Before we can understand who we are and why we do the things we do (psychology), we must first learn something about God (theology). So let's embark on a theological crash course in who God is and what he is like. Scripture tells us that we are beings made in the image of God.

Read Genesis 1:26 in the margin. We will be learning more about the meaning of this verse as the study continues, but for now, what does it mean to you to be made in God's image?

_____

_____

"Then God said, 'Let us make man in our image, in our likeness, and let them rule over the fish of the sea and the birds of the air, over the livestock, over all the earth, and over all the creatures that move along the ground.' "

—Genesis 1:26

That verse is a pretty striking statement, don't you agree? The God who created us made us not in the image of angels or other celestial beings but in His own image. We are bearers of the divine image. The Almighty paid us the highest compliment He could when He designed us after Himself.

What does it mean to be made in God's image? The central idea behind the word *image* is similarity. There are ways in which we are similar to God and ways in which we are dissimilar. Take first some of the dissimilarities. God is all powerful; we are not. God is all wise; we are not. God is everywhere present; we are not. Those are ways in which we are unlike Him.

Now consider the ways in which we are like God. God is a personal being who relates. So are we. God is a rational being who thinks. So are we. God is an emotional being who feels. So are we. God is a volitional being who chooses. So are we. When He designed His human creation, He copied these elements into us.

We must learn something else about God. First, we would know nothing about God unless He had taken the initiative to make Himself known. Second, though we may know something about God, we will never be able to know everything about Him. If God were not too big for our minds, He would be too small for our hearts.

It is one thing to say that God cannot be fully known and quite another to say that God cannot be known at all. I have always liked the story of the five-year-old girl who rushed up to her newly born brother in his hospital room, leaned over him, and said, "Quick, tell me, what is God like?" She was bitterly disappointed when all the newborn infant did was make a few gurgling sounds, roll his eyes, and fall into a deep sleep.

Having overheard her parents say he had just come from heaven, the little girl shrewdly figured out that he might have some inside information. That girl expressed in her own way the deepest hope of the deepest souls who have ever lived: what is God like?

Common misconceptions about God conceal His true nature.
Underline the impressions of God you have held in the past.

Doting grandfather	Absentee father	Santa Claus
Mean old grouch	Policeman	Judge

God Is a Personal Being Who Relates.

Have you ever thought about the fact that the very first thing revealed about God in the Bible is that He is a relational being? Look again in the margin at that majestic verse with which the Bible begins.

"In the beginning God created the heavens and the earth."

—Genesis 1:1

Who is the first person we meet when we open the Bible at its first page? God. The Hebrew word for God in that opening verse of Genesis is *Elohim,* which is in fact a plural word. The opening statement hints that more than one person is in the Godhead. Genesis 1:26 reinforces that thought: "Then God said, 'Let us make man in our image, in our likeness, and let them rule over the fish of the sea and the birds of the air, over the livestock, over all the earth, and over all the creatures that move along the ground.' "

To whom was God speaking when He said, " 'Let us' "? Most evangelical theologians are one on this thought: He was speaking to the other members of the Trinity. One of the great mysteries of our faith that no one can fully comprehend is that God is one yet three persons: Father, Son, and Holy Spirit.

Not only is there society in the Godhead, but it is a perfect society. Sometimes we find it difficult to get along with people for a few days, but the Trinity have been relating throughout all eternity and have never had a quarrel or disagreement. God is a personal being who exists eternally in a relationship among persons. He is His own community.

Therefore, when humans were created, they were designed as relational beings. Adam was created first. As God looked down on him all alone in the garden, He concluded, " 'It is not good for the man to be alone. I will make a helper suitable for him' " (Gen. 2:18).

Before sin entered the garden, the first couple, Adam and Eve, related to one another in perfect harmony and thus were microcosms of the Deity. They related to one another on earth as the Trinity related to one another in heaven—perfectly, with no dissension.

In heaven, we will not be discussing truth or doctrine. We will relate in the same way God relates—beautifully, perfectly, eternally. No arguments, no quarrels, no dissension. Whatever else the three Persons of the Trinity do, nothing can be more important than the fact that they maintain within and among themselves perfect, other-centered relationships. That, then, is **the first aspect of God we must consider—God relates.**

Why is it still important to God that His earthly children get along? Read the verses below and write your answer in the space provided.

John 13:34 _____

Philippians 2:2 _____

I John 4:11-12 _____

I John 4:19-21 _____

God Is a Rational Being Who Thinks.

The second characteristic of God which he shared with His original creation is this: the ability to think. The statement that God thinks may seem too obvious to be stated, but some persons claim that this is not a rationally-based universe and things happen by chance or by random. Scripture leaves us no doubt that God thinks. I could bring a host of Scriptures to prove that point, but let Isaiah 55:8 suffice.

Consider the famous axiom: Wherever there is a thing, there must have been a preceding thought, and where there is a thought, there must have been a thinker. Most everyone is familiar with the famous saying attributed to Descartes: "I think therefore I am." One of my teachers used to tell the story that one day Descartes stepped into a sidewalk cafe in Paris and the waiter asked him, "Would you like coffee, sir?"

Descartes hesitated for a moment and said, "I think not," and immediately disappeared. Let the apostle Paul have the last word on this point: " 'Who has known the mind of the Lord? Or who has been his counselor?' " (Rom. 11:34).

When God made Adam and Eve in the beginning, He endued them with the capacity to think. Follow for a moment how God engaged His mind with the mind of Adam in the garden. Read Genesis 2:16-17 in the margin.

With this God-given ability to think, Adam was able to plan, tend the garden, and later see his thought processes actually at work when God invited him to name all the animals of creation. This is how Scripture puts it: "Now the Lord God had formed out of the ground all the beasts of the field and all the birds of the air. He brought them to the man to see what he would name them; and whatever the man called each living creature, that was its name. So the man gave names to all the livestock, the birds of the air and all the beasts of the field" (Gen. 2:19).

" 'My thoughts are not your thoughts, neither are your ways my ways,' declares the Lord."

—ISAIAH 55:8

"The Lord God commanded the man, 'You are free to eat from any tree in the garden; but you must not eat from the tree of the knowledge of good and evil, for when you eat of it you will surely die.' "

—GENESIS 2:16-17

God asked Adam to name the animals because (check one or more):
❑ God just couldn't think of any names.
❑ Adam was more creative.
❑ Adam had more time.
❑ God was transferring responsibility for the care
of the animals to Adam.
❑ God was preparing Adam for Eve's arrival.

God did not name the animals but brought them to Adam to see what he would name them. I believe Adam's sinless mind would have been so insightful that he would have given the right names to the animals, names that summed up their characteristics.

By the way, this is the first time we see Adam speaking. Speech requires words. Thoughts are sentences we put together. Clearly his thought processes were at work, his mind alert and functioning perfectly as he named the animals and brought them under his authority. Shortly there-after, God put the rational capacity of Adam to work when he met his mate for the first time.

How did Adam realize that the woman standing before him had come from a part of his flesh? Presumably, his mind was perfectly receptive to the divine mind. God's thoughts, I imagine, mingled with his thoughts in a way that was difficult to tell where one began and the other ended. The ability of God to think and to think clearly about everything was conveyed to Adam in the act of his original creation. We shall see in more detail later that the same ability was evident also in Eve. **The second divine characteristic is—God thinks.**

God Is an Emotional Being Who Feels.

Some theologians throughout history have argued that God is not moved by emotions. This is nonsense of course. The Bible is full of statements and word pictures that show God to be an emotional being.

Perhaps you have not considered that God has emotions. Match these verses with God's feelings at that moment.
____ 1. Grief and pain   a. Exodus 34:14
____ 2. Jealousy   b. Genesis 6:6-7
____ 3. Anger   c. Numbers 32:13

The Almighty chooses the relationship between lovers to describe His rela-tionship with mankind. The Old Testament abounds with husband-bride imagery. God woos his people and dotes on them, and when they ignore Him, He feels spurned like a jilted lover.

Read the following Scriptures and write how each describes God.

Jeremiah 31:3 _____

Hosea 2:19-20 _____

Hosea 11:1 _____

"We do not have a high priest who is unable to sympathize with our weaknesses, but we have one who has been tempted in every way, just as we are— yet was without sin."

—HEBREWS 4:15

The emotional life of the Deity is beyond our power to fully understand. How can we comprehend, for example, that the Lord hears the prayers of millions of saints every day, some who are in deep pain, yet He is able to sympathize with every one (Heb. 4:15)? Some will be brokenhearted, disconsolate, weighed down, while others will be filled with joy. How can God weep with those who weep and rejoice with those who rejoice in such measure? And all this without taking a break to gather His resources?

Who can comprehend it indeed? But we believe it because He says so. If we could comprehend it, then we would be as God. God's infinite nature can't be penetrated by human beings. Just as God's thoughts are beyond our full comprehension (Isa. 55:9), so are His emotions. Though we do not fully understand them, we know that He has these emotions. **The third divine characteristic is—God feels.**

When God created Adam and Eve, He gave them the ability to feel emotions. A good illustration of emotions at work is Adam's reaction to the arrival of Eve into his life. God put Adam to sleep, we are told, took from his side a piece of flesh, and built a woman around that. Then when Adam awoke and saw her, he burst into poetry. Can anything provoke more feeling than a poem? Granted, the words in our English Bible don't sound like poetry, but in Hebrew that is exactly what they are. Listen to them again:

> *The man said, "This is now bone of my bones*
> *and flesh of my flesh;*
> *she shall be called 'woman,'*
> *for she was taken out of man" (Gen. 2:23).*

Hebrew poetry is difficult to translate into English. The Hebrew words are lilting. Keep in mind that the last thing Adam saw before he was put to sleep was animals. The first thing he saw when he awoke was Eve, someone like himself yet different. What emotion must have surged through him when he saw her standing before him? This paraphrase might convey something of the passion that would have arisen within him: "And Adam said, Wow! At last this is someone I can relate to. This beats anything I have seen in the animal creation. I feel closer to this being than anything I have yet seen. She was taken out of me but now is alongside me. I can't wait to get to know her better."

Trust me, that may not be a a literal translation, but that's the kind of thing that went through Adam's mind and affected his emotions as he saw for the first time the woman who was to be his wife.

God built into His human creation that same ability to express feelings.

Do you find it easier to express negative or positive emotions?
❏ Negative ❏ Positive

This week set a goal for yourself. Intentionally express an emotion that you would usually suppress or deny, leaning on Christ's power to express it in a responsible way. Write the results below.

_____

_____

God Is a Volitional Being Who Chooses.

Christians may differ about the length of the days for creation, but Bible believers are unanimous in the fact that God created the world by an act of His will. Repeatedly in the first chapter of Genesis we read, "God said." Whatever God said came to pass because it was an expression of His will. If there is any doubt about this, then all we have to do is turn to the book of Revelation where the worshipping hosts cry:

> *"You are worthy, our Lord and God,*
> *to receive glory and honor and power,*
> *for you created all things,*
> *and by your will they were created*
> *and have their being" (Rev. 4:11).*

Read Job 38:4-18, which is part of God's answer to Job's questions about his predicament. As you read, note in the margin the actions of God in creation.

Actions of God in Creation

God chooses, and His choices are made with the good of the universe in mind. " 'I know the plans I have for you,' declares the Lord, 'plans to prosper you and not to harm you, plans to give you hope and a future' " (Jer. 29:11). A host of Scriptures could be brought together to show that God is a choosing being. Here are just a few:

> *"God chose the foolish things of the world to shame the wise;*
> *God chose the weak things of the world to shame the strong"*
> *(1 Cor. 1:27).*

> " *'If you belonged to the world, it would love you as its own.*
> *As it is, you do not belong to the world, but I have chosen*
> *you out of the world. That is why the world hates you' "*
> *(John 15:19).*

The fourth characteristic is—God chooses. How was the characteristic of volition played out in the first human pair? Look again at the account of Adam naming the animals. Adam was no puppet or ventriloquist's dummy. We saw a few minutes ago how his sinless mind would have read the characteristics of the animals and given them the right names. The choice of each name was his.

Here was Adam's volitional capacity being put to work. In effect God was saying, "All these animals are under your authority. When you name something, you bring it under your authority. Whatever you call it, Adam, that will be its name." In relation to the woman, it was not God who named her but Adam. Her name means *mother of all living*.

Another aspect of Adam and Eve's ability to choose is in the command given to them in Genesis 1:28. Adam and Eve were given the prerogative of ruling over the earth, of being creative in it as God was their Creator. Ruling means action—not just reaction, and action implies choice.

God placed Adam and Eve in the midst of a wondrous creation. The environment in which they found themselves had not yet realized all its potential. It awaited the touch of Adam and Eve in cooperation with God for its realization.

It has been said that filling the earth with people is the only command of God that mankind has faithfully kept! In what ways do you feel humans have been responsible rulers of the earth? Irresponsible? Check the appropriate column.

	Responsible	Irresponsible
Food supply	▦	▦
Ozone layer	▦	▦
Water quality	▦	▦
Air quality	▦	▦
Reforesting	▦	▦
Endangered species	▦	▦
Other?_____	▦	▦

One more illustration is perhaps needed to show Adam and Eve's faculty of choice. In Genesis 2:16-17 we read: "The Lord God commanded the man, 'You are free to eat from any tree in the garden; but you must not eat from the tree of the knowledge of good and evil, for when you eat of it you will surely die.' "

Clearly, Adam and Eve were placed in circumstances of probation. In the garden of His activity, God marked the limit of man's possibility by two sacramental symbols—both were trees. One was the tree of life of which they were commanded to eat; the other was the tree of knowledge of good and evil of which they were commanded not to eat. Finite will was to be tested by keeping the commands of God. It was for them to choose. They could do what God asked, or they could disobey. The choice was theirs.

The picture we have of Adam and Eve in the garden of Eden is of two people created in the image of God, living in dependency and union with God, cooperating in activity with God. Adam and Eve were functioning as microcosms of the Deity on earth but with one difference. The image of God was in a physical body. God is not a physical being, but when He made mankind, He made them not only as spiritual but material beings also.

"God blessed them and said to them, 'Be fruitful and increase in number; fill the earth and subdue it. Rule over the fish of the sea and the birds of the air and over every living creature that moves on the ground.' "

—Genesis 1:28

Some have said that the end of all God's purposes in His creation is embodiment. In a material universe God put the image of Himself in a human frame so that they could function on earth in a body as God functions in heaven without body—relating, thinking, feeling, and willing.

The fact that the image of God functions in our frail human bodies is extremely important, and we shall look at this in more detail later.

In this session we have said four pivotal things.
1. God is a personal being who relates.
2. God is a rational being who thinks.
3. God is an emotional being who feels.
4. God is a volitional being who chooses.

That same design can be seen reflected in His human creation, for Adam and Eve were made in God's image.

> Like God, they could relate.
> Like God, they could think.
> Like God, they could feel.
> Like God, they could choose.

However, disaster struck that beautiful environment. We will look at the details of that next week.

Knowing God Personally

Let the last thoughts in week 1 be this: Although it is possible to know something about God through the study of His attributes, it is not possible to know God intimately until one experiences what the Bible calls *a new birth*.

During Jesus' time on this earth, He met with a leading religious scholar named Nicodemus. Though Nicodemus had great religious knowledge, he had not the slightest notion of what Jesus was talking about when our Lord said, " ' "You must be born again" ' " (John 3:7). The Apostle Paul made the same point in 1 Corinthians 2:14. Read it in the margin.

How does someone go about knowing God personally? Turn to page 116-117 in this book and follow the path that is laid out for you there.

I once counseled a professor with four Ph.D's, including one in theology. As we talked about God, he asked me several times to repeat what I had said, offering this explanation. "I can grapple with many scientific theories, but understanding God is beyond me." Our conversations were radically different after he was converted and came into the experience which Jesus called *the new birth*. He understood and saw God differently because he knew God personally.

Only a personal encounter with God through His Son Jesus Christ can initiate you into a spiritual world where you pass from *knowing about Him* to *knowing Him for who He is*. We are made in His divine image. We will return next week to that awesome subject.

"The man without the Spirit does not accept the things that come from the Spirit of God, for they are foolishness to him, and he cannot understand them, because they are spiritually discerned."

—1 CORINTHIANS 2:14

Learning from the Mistakes of Others

King David's affair. Simon Peter's denial. Noah's drunkenness. Abraham's adultery with Hagar. Jacob's conniving. God's Word doesn't spare the details when it comes to revealing the failures of His children.

Why doesn't God spare the blushes of His people who fell by the wayside? Romans 15:4 explains: "Everything that was written in the past was written to teach us, so that through endurance and the encouragement of the Scriptures we might have hope." God wants us to learn from the mistakes of others. However, we will not be able to do that by just reading about them; we must take time to study them carefully.

One of the most powerful ways of bringing home the truth of what is being said in the video seminar is to see these truths and concepts illustrated in the life of a Bible character. Biographies have a different effect on us than any other type of literature. Couched in story form, they disarm suspicion, cut through our denials and rationalizations, and the truth glides into our minds without our realizing what is happening. Biographies reach out with invisible hands and say, "Look what is happening in the life of this person; is the same thing happening to you?"

God wants to make us experts in the art of living. Biographies show us both how to live and how not to live. One of the ways in which the records of some Bible characters serve us is to show us how the image of God went so badly wrong in their lives. We should not be surprised to discover the five areas of functioning in the lives of Bible characters, for everyone has been made in the image of God. People deny that image when they pursue unbiblical goals based on a wrong understanding of what brings them security, self-worth, and significance.

A Fascinating Biblical Case Study

One Bible character who clearly illustrates how God's image in him went so badly wrong is King Saul. So much biographical material is given to us about King Saul in Scripture that we will have no difficulty in identifying his wrong goals, his dominant problem emotion, his wrong thinking, and his relational style. Allow this case study to become a mirror for you.

King Saul could have thrived as the first king of Israel. Regrettably, however, his life ended in tragic circumstances. Let's remind ourselves of how he came to be King. The beginning of the story is told for us in 1 Samuel 8:1-22. Before you read it, consider this: God wanted Israel to experience the blessings of living under a theocracy, that is, under the direct rule and government of God. By the end of the period of Judges they had degenerated into moral and social anarchy.

The people asked for a king so that they could be like other nations. Reluctantly, God agreed to their request. Their intentions in wanting a king were opposite to God's intentions. They wanted to be like other nations; He wanted them to be unlike other nations. The request for a king to come from a theocratically established nation—living directly under God's rule—was tantamount to rejecting God as King (1 Sam. 8:7). Samuel warned the people of how oppressive and self-serving a king would become. Some commentators believe that it was as a judgment that God conceded to their demands.

Imagine yourself to be Saul's spiritual director. Armed with the information you have been given concerning the image of God in mankind, consider the five areas of King Saul's functioning (relational, rational, emotional, volitional, and physical). Your assignment over the next seven weeks is to come to some conclusions about how God's image in this man was defaced. Then you will be asked to give a tentative diagnosis of Saul. What personality problems serve as five keys that explain King Saul's behavior? We will explore each of them in coming weeks.

---

[1]James Mallory, *The Kink & I* (Wheaton: Victor Books, 1975), 29.
[2]Ibid.

Session 2: How It All Went Wrong

∾

Introduction

God laid down a beautiful plan for Adam and Eve in the garden of Eden; each ideally related to God and then to each other. But the unthinkable happened. They chose to tamper with God's plan for their relationship with Him and each other.

1. The beautiful garden of Eden was an ideal environment for the first human

   pair, but there was one _____ off limits (Gen. 2:16-17).

2. The prohibition was there for a number of reasons but one in particular: would

   they _____ or _____?

3. The devil's strategy can be seen in the way he instilled _____ in Eve's mind.

4. How we _____ affects the way we _____, and how we _____

   affects the way we _____.

5. Our personalities are made up of (at least) three parts: _____,

   _____, and _____.

6. Note the focus of the devil's attack:

   First, God's _____. Second, God's _____.

   "The root of sin is the suspicion that God is not good" (Oswald Chambers).[1]

7. _____ of God led to _____ of God, and _____ of

   God led to _____ toward God.

Once we comprehend the satanic strategy that lay behind Adam and Eve's capitulation, we are able to better understand the design of the personality and how it can be used as a force for good or for evil.

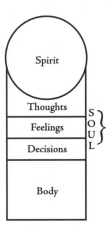

8. Eve took the fruit and ate it and also gave some to her husband, who was

   _____ _____ (see Gen. 3:6).

9. Consider the long-term consequences of Adam and Eve's sin:

   for Adam: Genesis 3:17-19; for Eve: Genesis 3:16.

10. Adam and Eve's sin was a _____, _____,

    _____, _____, and _____ disaster.

By putting an angel with a flaming sword on the east side of Eden, God made sure they would not have access to the tree of life and live forever in their sinful condition. If they were to know God and experience Him, then the answer must lie in another direction than east of Eden.

How It All Went Wrong

"All have sinned and fall short of the glory of God,
and are justified freely by his grace through the
redemption that came by Christ Jesus."

ROMANS 3:23

Without doubt, Adam and Eve lived in a perfect world—no sin, no disturbance of spirit, no suffering, no shame. The Almighty declared it "very good," but not for long.

Many theorists have tried to explain sin away. They will say:

- You are stuck somewhere on the hierarchy of needs.
- You are genetically wired toward aggression and anger.
- Raging hormones are the culprit.
- Psychic impulses conflict with the dictates of society.
- You are Aries with Jupiter rising.
- You are demon possessed.
- You have no will power.
- You are having an identity crisis.
- Your self-talk gets you into trouble.
- You are a victim of a traumatic childhood experience.

This week we will discover how it all went wrong, how the perfect couple in the perfect environment became magnificent ruins.

As you read, ask yourself these questions:
1. In a nutshell, what was the original sin?
2. How did it affect Adam and Eve?
3. What are the implications for me?

What a beautiful plan God put into action in the garden of Eden with the first human pair! Each ideally related to God, then to each other. Adam was no tyrant; he was a strong, confident leader and lover. And Eve was no intellectual pygmy. She was bright, alert, radiant, regal, and passionately alive. They wore no masks and had no barriers between them—no concealment of their bodies or souls.

Imagine this problem-free environment. List some descriptive words in the margin.

The Nature of Temptation

Then the unthinkable happened. They chose to tamper with God's plan for their relationship with Him and with each another. As a result, the divine image became fragmented and defaced. In order to understand how this happened, we need to take a closer look at that perfect world in which Adam and Eve lived.

Scripture gives us a picture of unimaginable beauty and loveliness in Eden's pristine environment. The garden was filled with trees of all descriptions, bearing, we assume, the most luscious fruits. Adam and Eve could eat from any of the trees of the garden with one exception. The issue of that specific tree was extremely significant. In a non-negotiable command, God labeled one tree off-limits. Adam could not possibly have misunderstood. Read in the margin what the Almighty said to him.

" 'You are free to eat from any tree in the garden; but you must not eat from the tree of the knowledge of good and evil, for when you eat of it you will surely die.' "
—Genesis 2:16-17

Throughout the ages and since the book of Genesis was written, many have speculated on what this prohibition was all about. In my view the issue was this: would they obey or disobey God's command?

One theologian I know describes the situation in relation to the tree like this: "Imagine" he says, "you are sitting in a large library where no one else than the librarian is present. The librarian says to you, 'I have to go out for half an hour. You can look at every book you want to, but there is one book, right there on the top shelf, all by itself, you must not look at. It contains important information that relates to you but is not necessary for you to know. If you do dip into it, you will be expelled from this library and never allowed to enter it again.' "

Once the librarian had gone, what would you do? The issue is now whether you are willing to obey. A similar situation faced Adam and Eve in relation to God's command. They chose to disobey rather than to obey. As a result, the once innocent creation now knew chaos.

When Adam and Eve sinned, the ripple effect touched all of creation. Circle the ripple effect of your sin.

my self-esteem

my family influence

my witness to others

my church leadership

Other _____

The Process of Temptation

How did it all go wrong? It's a story that is all too familiar, but look with me again at the details of this sad episode which recounts the downfall of our first parents. The Tempter, Satan, entered the garden with a plan to bring about the downfall. The Devil approached Eve, not as a creature of ugliness but in the form of a serpent. He came disguised. There was seemingly nothing about him to be dreaded. Second Corinthians 11:14 helps us to understand something of his cunning and craftiness: "Satan himself masquerades as an angel of light."

When we read the account of the temptation of the first human pair in the Book of Genesis, remember that we are watching a scene that took place before the fall and before the serpent was cursed and consigned to crawling on its belly across the ground. The serpent was a beautiful creature, and there was nothing about it that would have made Eve afraid.

I find it very interesting that when the Devil came to tempt Eve, he didn't drag chains behind him and say, "I have come to damn your soul." He never tried to talk her into becoming an atheist. He talked theology; he talked about God: "He said to the woman, 'Did God really say, "You must not eat from any tree in the garden"?' " (Gen 3:1).

What a perfect conversation opener—his words were neither threatening nor intimidating. He left nothing for Eve to argue with in that statement. If I were to paraphrase it, it would read something like this: "My, this is a beautiful garden is it not? And you are free to eat of all this?" Eve replied, "Yes, we can eat of every tree in this garden except that one over there, the tree of knowledge of good and evil. God said if we ate of that one, we would surely die and we must not touch it."

Harold Robbins, in a sermon he calls "A Case Study in Temptation," makes an interesting point in relation to Eve's statement. "God didn't say anything about touching it [the tree]. Some people defend God by becoming stricter than God. They not only know God's commands, but they believe they are holier if they go beyond those commands. There is destruction in that. Eve says, 'You know we can't taste it, we can't even touch it.' What Satan had done of course, was to focus her mind on that single tree, the one thing prohibited."[2]

Read Matthew 23:23-26. Underline how the Pharisees added to God's laws. Did Jesus commend them for their righteousness? ❏ Yes ❏ No

Let's focus for a few moments on the words from Genesis 2:17: " 'You will surely die.' " In Hebrew it reads like this: "Dying, you shall die." I take that to mean that the moment you eat of the fruit of that tree you will die spiritually and begin to die physically. That's the thought suggested in the words as they appear in the original language. The question is often asked: If Adam and Eve had not eaten of the fruit of the tree of the knowledge of good and evil, would they have lived forever? I believe so—as long as they had access to the tree of life.

" 'Woe to you, teachers of the law and Pharisees, you hypocrites! You give a tenth of your spices— mint, dill and cummin. But you have neglected the more important matters of the law— justice, mercy and faithfulness. You should have practiced the latter, without neglecting the former. You blind guides! You strain out a gnat but swallow a camel.

Woe to you, teachers of the law and Pharisees, you hypocrites! You clean the outside of the cup and dish, but inside they are full of greed and self-indulgence. Blind Pharisee! First clean the inside of the cup and dish, and then the outside also will be clean.' "

—MATTHEW 23:23-26

The Root of Sin

The Devil then set about attacking God's word by suggesting that God was not speaking the truth when He told them they would die. "You will not surely die," the serpent said to the woman. "For God knows that when you eat of it your eyes will be opened, and you will be like God, knowing good and evil" (Gen. 3:4-5).

The statement of the serpent, " 'You will not surely die,' " is based on a lie. When the Devil said these words, I often wonder if he threw back his head, laughed uproariously, and thus conveyed by his body language this idea: "Oh come on now, surely you don't believe that anything like that will happen, do you—that you will surely die? All over a bit of fruit? Notice how he insinuated doubt into her mind. His very clever plan followed the design of the personality. Our personalities work like this: Our thoughts affect the way we feel and how we feel affects the way we act.

Give an example of how your thoughts affect your feelings and how your feelings affect your actions.

Thought	Feeling	Action

Consider how it works. As thoughts drop into our minds, what we think about affects the way we feel. In turn, how we feel affects the way we act. Doubt of God leads to dislike of God. Dislike of God leads in turn to disobedience toward God. The personality capitulates and the battle is won.

Whatever the elusive term *personality* means, the least it means is that it is made up of three things: thought, feeling, and will. When we talk about a person, we mean someone who can think, feel, and act. That is the irreducible minimum. As doubt of God leads to dislike of God and dislike of God leads to disobedience toward God, the soul is invaded with a simple yet very effective strategy.

Satan's attack was not just an attack on God's word but an attack on His character. Look at the Tempter's words once again: " 'God knows that when you eat of it your eyes will be opened, and you will be like God, knowing good and evil' " (Gen. 3:5).

Satan's statement amounts to nothing more than slander, a direct attack on God's goodness. Satan tried to impress upon Eve that God was not as considerate and loving as He appeared to be, or else He would not have limited her freedom. The implication behind his words was this: God wants to limit your freedom and stop you from reaching your full potential. He wants to keep you from the joy and pleasure that could be ahead of you. If you eat that fruit you will become like Him, knowing good and evil. You will have experiences that you never thought were possible.

Oswald Chambers transformed my whole understanding of the original temptation. I shall never forget reading his statement that, "the root of sin is the suspicion that God is not good."[3] Until I had read that I thought the root of sin was rebellion, but Oswald Chambers with a thrust of his rapier-like logic sees deep into the heart of the situation.

"The root of sin is the suspicion that God is not good."

The Devil knew better than Eve how her personality was constructed. He knew that once Eve entertained a doubt about God's goodness and allowed it to simmer in her mind, it would not be long before that doubt would lead to dislike of God and ultimately to disobedience.

Have you or has someone close to you followed this same pattern?

Doubt of God _____

Dislike of God _____

Disobedience to God _____

If so, what was the result? _____

_____

I saw this statement quoted in a magazine some time ago: "When God looks bad, sin looks good."

Think with me about this interesting verse: "When the woman saw that the fruit of the tree was good for food and pleasing to the eye, and also desirable for gaining wisdom, she took some and ate it. She also gave some to her husband, who was with her, and he ate it. Then the eyes of both of them were opened, and they realized they were naked; so they sewed fig leaves together and made coverings for themselves" (Gen. 3:6).

One of our British Bible teachers, Dr. Campbell Morgan, gives us one of the most illuminating insights into the design of the personality that I have ever read. He throws a beam of light on how temptation proceeds and how the personality capitulates.

Once Eve's thinking and feelings began to change, she looked at the tree in a new way and through different eyes. She had listened to the lie of the tempter and then new desires began to take control. Her senses became alive to what was forbidden. The thing that was once out of bounds and caused her no problem then became something to be desired. Once God and His word were doubted and rejected, her senses quickly become alive to evil. The next thing we read is: "She took [the fruit] and ate it" (Gen. 3:6), but the matter did not end there: "She also gave some to her husband, who was with her, and he ate it" (Gen. 3:6).

> Once God and His word were doubted and rejected, her senses quickly become alive to evil.

Why didn't Adam speak up? Check one or more.
❑ He was in another part of the garden.
❑ He was curious to see what would happen.
❑ Like Eve he was deceived.
❑ He thought only Eve would get the blame.
❑ Other? _____

For Want of a Word

Many people believe that Eve took of the forbidden fruit and then went searching for Adam to give him some too. The Hebrew text is quite clear, however. Adam was standing at Eve's side when she was tempted. Apparently as the temptation proceeded he said nothing. This simple but indicting phrase has largely been ignored by theologians, but it shouldn't be.

Why didn't Adam speak up and remind Eve what God had said concerning the tree of the knowledge of good and evil: "You must not eat from the tree, for when you eat of it, you shall surely die" (Gen. 2:17)? Here on earth, we will never know. Scripture doesn't tell us why Adam remained silent, but my guess is Adam allowed his curiosity to overpower his reason. He was not deceived as Eve was. One thing, however, is clear: he failed God and his wife by not speaking in that crucial moment.

Dr. Larry Crabb believes Adam's disobedience did not begin with his eating but with his silence. "It was a silent man," he says, "who eventually broke God's clear command."[4] He says also that just as Adam failed God and his wife by his silence, the same failure is repeated again and again in marital relationships. A fuller quote on this subject comes from his book *The Silence of Adam:* "Like every man, I am silent just like Adam was silent. Sometimes I stand dumbfounded in the face of my confusion. When my wife asks me to share even the smallest part of myself, I occasionally bristle. When she cries, I may become angry with her. Her tears frighten me, because I don't know what to do with them. When she tells me I have done something wrong, I defend myself to the bitter end. If she finds fault with me, I find ten things wrong with her. I refuse to be wrong. I use words, I speak; but I use words to destroy relationship—as the serpent did in the garden."[5]

Several years ago I spoke at a five-day conference to ministers in Moscow on the theme "The Theology and Psychology of Marriage." In that address I referred to Adam's silence and how it contributed to the downfall of the first human pair.

In the audience was a woman, a Russian poet, who was so intrigued by the idea of Adam's silence that overnight she wrote a poem entitled "For Want of a Word." When through an interpreter she read it to me, I invited her to share it with the whole conference. Never will I forget the impact the poem made on that audience, particularly the last line. It hung in the air and for minutes no one moved as they caught the dramatic importance of what was being said: "For want of a word Paradise was lost."

We would do well to ponder the words again: "She took [the fruit] and ate it. She also gave some to her husband, who was with her" (Gen. 3:6). This statement is the root of all our troubles.

When have you been silent at a time spoken words would have been more appropriate?

"She took [the fruit] and ate it. She also gave some to her husband, who was with her."

—Genesis 3:6

The Birth of the Clothing Industry

"Then the eyes of both of them were opened, and they realized they were naked; so they sewed fig leaves together and made coverings for themselves."

—GENESIS 3:7

"Then the man and his wife heard the sound of the Lord God as he was walking in the garden in the cool of the day, and they hid from the Lord God among the trees of the garden."

—GENESIS 3:8

"The Lord God called to the man, 'Where are you?' "

—GENESIS 3:9

Up until that moment Adam and Eve had not been conscious of their nakedness. They lived in perfect and unpretentious innocence, enjoying the delights and intimacies of the relationship without concern for their nudity. I believe their nakedness was not only physical but mental and emotional as well. Just as there were no physical barriers between them there were no mental or emotional barriers either. Immediately after they had eaten the fruit, however, they became self conscious and were obviously concerned as to how they appeared to each other.

The most famous cover up in history was not Watergate, says a friend of mine, but the one that took place in Eden. They hid not only from each other but also from God. "It was at this moment," said a quaint old North of England preacher, "that there took place the birth of the clothing industry."

Read Genesis 3:8 in the margin. Isn't that interesting? Having partaken of the forbidden fruit and allowed sin to enter their lives, their whole behavior changed. Whereas previously I imagine they ran to keep their daily appointment with God, now they ran away from him. But though they ran, God sought them.

Genesis 3:9 contains the first question God asked in the Bible: where are you? It really is rhetorical because God knew the answer. What He was saying was, "why are you hiding from Me? You have never run away from Me before. Why now? I made your hearts for intimacy with Me, but you have given your heart to another." Many know the pain of a love affair that turns to immobilizing pain as one realizes that a lover could leave for another.

Why did God ask him a question when he knew the answer? The point was to surface an admission of his guilt. But Adam gave two reasons for his flight from the Almighty. He was afraid, and he was naked.

What are we to make of the words, " 'I was naked' " (Gen. 3:10)? That plea may seem strange to us today because we have never experienced true innocence. Children experience it to a certain degree, but it does not last long; once self-consciousness develops, there is a strong antipathy to being seen naked. From that day to this, it is a natural reaction with most people to cover themselves when they are naked.

Following hard on the heels of the first question comes a second: " 'Who told you that you were naked?' " (Gen. 3:11). And before Adam had a chance to reply, the Almighty asked: " 'Have you eaten from the tree that I commanded you not to eat from?' " (Gen. 3:11).

Have you ever thought about this? Why did God ask Adam a question when he knew the answer perfectly well? Had not the Almighty (who is omniscient, all-seeing) witnessed the scene when both Adam and Eve had eaten the forbidden fruit? Yes, of course, but the point of the question was to get Adam to own up to the act of disobedience. They could only deal with the problem after it had been exposed.

How does God usually confront you about your sin?
❑ Holy Spirit's quiet nudging
❑ Guilty conscience
❑ Prayer
❑ Christian music
❑ Sermons
❑ Bible study
❑ Other Christians

God's confrontation of Adam and Eve is one of the unforgettable dialogues in Scripture. Adam replies: " 'The woman you put here with me—she gave me some fruit from the tree, and I ate it' " (Gen. 3:12).

Notice once again the evasion: Adam seems to imply that if God had not given him the woman, trouble would not have arisen. Instead of saying, "God, I'm sorry. I'm guilty as charged," Adam attempts to put the blame on the woman. A paraphrase would read like this: "God, the woman you gave me has caused all this trouble. I ate this because of what you did and what she did."

God doesn't argue with him but next confronts Eve, who must have been "shaking in her apron of leaves," as Charles Swindoll puts it.[6] " 'What is this you have done?' The woman said, 'The serpent deceived me, and I ate' " (Gen. 3:13).

What a perfect picture this is of what psychologists describe as projection, off-loading the blame onto another. As one wag put it, "Adam blamed his wife, his wife blamed the serpent, and the serpent didn't have a leg to stand on." They seemed to be capable of anything rather than face up to the fact that they were guilty as charged.

The blame game is still fiercely fought in the battle of the sexes. Choose an appropriate response.
❑ Take the whole load of guilt. Everything was your fault.
❑ Blame others, but sound convincing. Act hurt that you were even a suspect.
❑ Get there first with the accusations. It throws others off guard.
❑ The strong silent type just doesn't want to talk about it.
❑ There is a better way. Read Ephesians 4:29-32.

A better way is _____.

Consequences of Sin

God condemned the serpent and consigned him to slithering across the ground. If we could have seen the beauty of the serpent in its pristine condition, we might better understand the judgment that fell on it. How different the serpent in the garden would have been from the ones we know today.

God then judged His creation in gender-specific ways.

> *To the woman he said,*
> *"I will greatly increase your pains in childbearing;*
> *with pain you will give birth to children.*
> *Your desire will be for your husband,*
> *and he will rule over you" (Gen. 3:16).*

Presumably, if Adam and Eve had not sinned the woman would have brought forth children without pain. Now, however, she is told that birth will be painful. Also He said, " 'your desire will be for your husband.' " What does that mean? It means that she would long for her husband to be the man God intended him to be—a loving leader—but that she would be disappointed because he would not come up to her expectations.

Have you seen this judgment ring true in male-female relationships? In what ways has it been a "curse" between them?

_____

_____

God's judgment on the man was this:

> *To Adam he said, "Because you listened to your wife and*
> *ate from the tree about which I commanded you, 'You must*
> *not eat of it,'*
> *"Cursed is the ground because of you;*
> *through painful toil you will eat of it*
> *all the days of your life.*
> *It will produce thorns and thistles for you,*
> *and you will eat the plants of the field.*
> *By the sweat of your brow*
> *you will eat your food*
> *until you return to the ground,*
> *since from it you were taken;*
> *for dust you are*
> *and to dust you will return" (Gen. 3:17-19).*

The divine judgment was designed to bring Adam and Eve to the place where they would realize they would not be able to live out their lives in the way God designed them without God's help.

List several examples of the effects of the curse on men at work.

_____

Do you think these effects only apply to work outdoors?
❏ Yes   ❏ No   ❏ Not sure

Their resistance in their personal and public lives would force them time and again to throw themselves on God's mercy and grace. The judgment, then, was not so much punishment as correction.

When are you most likely to throw yourself on God's mercy and grace?

_____

Do you recall when you last realized your dependence on God? Write about it below.

_____

_____

Dignity Versus Depravity

Some believe Adam and Eve to be fictional characters rather than real persons God created. The New Testament writers believed them to be real persons, and so did Christ. If there were no Adam and Eve, then there was no fall. If there were no fall, there would be no need of a Savior. If there were no fall, then the historic fabric of Christianity collapses like a house of cards.

Now strange as it may seem, the doctrine of the fall is one of the most flattering to humankind. It not only flattens us but flatters us, pointing at one and the same time to Adam and Eve's dignity and depravity.

Their dignity is that they were made in God's image; their depravity is that they defaced that image by their sin.

Let's return to the question we asked at the beginning of this session: How could something so beautiful go so wrong? Here's the story once again—in a nutshell.

A tempter came into the garden of Eden and through a cunning and crafty temptation successfully implanted a doubt in Eve's mind concerning the goodness of God which quickly translated to dislike and disobedience.

Having decided to live independently of God, Adam and Eve were cut off from union with Him. They passed into a sphere of living where their essential powers found no proper way to express themselves. They once reflected so gloriously the divine image but now they became like a broken lens reflecting broken light. Their knowledge of God became restricted, their emotions were degraded, and their will became distorted. There could only be one response from the Creator to such failure to live according to His will.

"He drove the man out" (Gen 3:24). The fall was a relational, rational, emotional, volitional, and physical disaster. The sin that took place inside them worked its way into their physical beings, and from that moment, without access to the tree of life, they began to die.

Review this story of dignity and depravity until you can tell it to another person. This is at the heart of our witness to unbelievers.

All the grief and sadness that has been seen and that we are now seeing in the universe can be traced back to that monumental day in the garden of Eden when Adam and Eve violated God's command. God made sure that Adam and Eve would not return to the garden by appointing an angel to bar their way. Here's how Scripture puts it: "After he drove the man out, he placed on the east side of the garden of Eden cherubim and a flaming sword flashing back and forth to guard the way to the tree of life" (Gen. 3:24).

By putting a bouncer on the east of Eden, God made sure they would not have access to the tree of life and live forever in their sinful condition. If they were to know God, then the answer must lie in another direction.

But which direction? That is what we will be covering in future sessions.

Learning from the Mistakes of Others

Last week you were challenged to find in the life of King Saul characteristics of God that are also revealed in Adam and Eve and every other human from that time forward. King Saul is a character study, if you will, of what Christ-empowered living is all about. Unfortunately, he is a negative character study.

When we first meet Saul in Scripture our attention is drawn to his physical proportions. "There was a Benjamite, a man of standing, whose name was Kish son of Abiel, the son of Zeror, the son of Becorath, the son of Aphiah of Benjamin. He had a son named Saul, an impressive young man without equal among the Israelites—a head taller than any of the others" (1 Sam. 9:1).

He was tall, strong, athletic, and handsome. Although physical problems can contribute to bad behavior, it would be unlikely in his case.

Keep in mind, however, that a good physical image does not necessarily mean a good self-image. Often the most beautiful women and the most handsome men carry within them an image that contradicts the way others see them.

Could it have been that despite his impressive outward appearance Saul felt inadequate on the inside?

Look at the text again: It talks about his father being a man of standing in that ancient society. Isn't it intriguing that in the very first reference we come across concerning Saul we find him standing in the shadow of his father? And what kind of man was his father? "A mighty man of power" (1 Sam. 9:1, NKJV).

Were those big shoes to fill? Did he feel small in comparison? Did the people say to him, "Saul, are you going to be like your father?" Was there subtle pressure put on him to measure up to his father's abilities?

A subsequent moment in Saul's life could give more credence to the idea that Saul might have been struggling with a negative self-image. Take a little time to read through 1 Samuel 9 and 10. Did you find these key ideas? The possibility that Saul had a low view of himself becomes more believable. In 1 Samuel 9:3 Saul went to look for his father's lost donkeys and met up with the prophet Samuel. Samuel anointed Saul for the purpose of leadership in Israel (1 Sam. 10:1).

Later, when the time came for Saul's coronation (1 Sam. 10:20-27), a strange thing occurred: all the tribes were gathered, but where was Saul? He was there, but in hiding.

> *So they inquired further of the Lord, "Has the man come here yet?"*
>
> *And the Lord said, "Yes, he has hidden himself among the baggage."*
>
> *They ran and brought him out, and as he stood among the people he was a head taller than any of the others. Samuel said to all the people, "Do you see the man the Lord has chosen? There is no one like him among all the people."*
>
> *Then the people shouted, "Long live the king!"*
> *(1 Sam. 10:22-24).*

Why did Saul hide? Could it have been out of a sense of deep inadequacy, fear of failure, a negative self-image, a feeling of not being up to the task? Clearly something was going on in Saul's inner being that needed correcting. Perhaps if someone had been able to intervene at this stage and help him understand how to root his security, self-worth, and significance in God, we might well be reading a different story.

---

[1]Oswald Chambers, as quoted in Selwyn Hughes, *Christ Empowered Living* (Nashville: Broadman & Holman, 2001), 40.
[2]Harold Robbins, "A Case Study in Temptation," as quoted in Hughes, *Christ Empowered Living,* 38.
[3]Oswald Chambers, as quoted in Hughes, *Christ Empowered Living,* 40.
[4]Larry Crabb, *The Silence of Adam* (Grand Rapids: Zondervan, 1995), 97.
[5]Ibid.
[6]Charles Swindoll, as quoted in Hughes, *Christ Empowered Living,* 47.

Session 3: The Effects of the Fall

∾

1. Adam and Eve, though defaced, still retained the _____ of God in their personalities. They could still think, feel, choose, and relate to one another, albeit not as effectively as they did prior to the fall.

2. Their defaced and broken image of God, however, was passed on to their offspring. Though they had originally been created in God's image and God's likeness, their own children were created in _____ _____.

3. Consider first the _____ aspects and effects of Adam and Eve's sin:

    a. Because we are built for relationships (first with God and then with others), if God is not _____ our souls then we will seek some other sources of satisfaction.

    b. God has put within us a yearning for Himself which might best be described by the word _____.

4. Three things are needed for a clear sense of identity:

    _____, _____ - _____, and

    _____.

    Security: _____ _____

    Self-worth: _____

    Significance: _____ _____

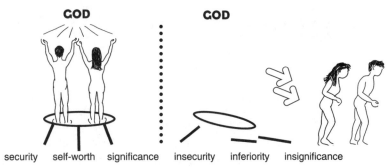

security   self-worth   significance   insecurity   inferiority   insignificance

5. The yearning to find _____ for our souls

   outside of God lies behind most problems of the personality.

6. The very first key to understanding how problems arise in the personality is

   _____ _____ _____.

7. Consider secondly, the _____ effects of Adam and Eve's original sin:

   Sin has affected our minds in a powerful way. Many Scriptures confirm this fact:

   _____   _____

   _____   _____

Adam and Eve exchanged the truth for a lie.

8. The _____: dependency on God for life and fulfillment

9. The _____: you can be a more fulfilled person by acting independently of God.

10. There is now a blindness in our minds. Our inability to figure out what life is

    all about is called in Scripture by the terms _____ or _____.

11. A key verse to understand is _____.

12. Truth requires that we give up vain attempts to make life work without _____.

13. The second reason why problems arise in the personality is because of

    _____ _____ _____.

THE EFFECTS OF THE FALL

❖

" 'The LORD himself goes before you and will be with you;
he will never leave you nor forsake you. Do not be afraid;
do not be discouraged.' "

DEUTERONOMY 31:8

We are meant to find a quality of joy and pleasure in the company of others
that is simply not available if we are alone. Therefore whatever threatens to
separate us provokes deep fear. In Who We Are and How We Relate, Larry
Crabb tells of his encounter with this terror in one of his counseling sessions.

Dr. Crabb relates that a single woman age 28 had offended everyone in
her community of friends. After being urged by a friend, she came to see
Larry. She knew her relationships were a mess. She insisted with consider-
able force, however, that the blame be divided between herself and the
insensitivity of others.

Ten minutes into their first session, she said, "I just want you to know
that I don't trust you—and I don't really see why I should."

He replied, "Trusting anyone would scare you to death." After twenty
more minutes of parrying, that comment opened her to talk tearfully about
her most passionate fantasy—a wonderfully terrifying daydream in which
she trusted someone with good results.

This woman was gripped by a paralyzing fear that if she ever presented
herself to people as the scared, desperate person she was, no one would be
willing to bear the weight of her desires. She could be abandoned or worse.
If she offered kindness to another—which she sometimes wanted to do—
it might be met with polite indifference.[1]

Reflect on how Adam and Eve must have felt there in the garden. They
were together but alone. They had lived together in perfect relationship—
no fears, nothing concealed, no suspicions—each enjoying what the other
had to give. Now they found themselves in an imperfect relationship beset
by fear, suspicion, and terror.

As you read, keep these questions in mind:

1. What were the direct and immediate consequences of Adam and Eve's
   sin on their relationship?
2. What were the direct and immediate consequences of Adam and Eve's
   sin on their rational abilities?
3. What consequences of sin do you recognize in your relationships and
   thinking processes?

The history of the human race can be summed up in four concise phrases:
- Mankind formed
- Mankind deformed
- Mankind informed
- Mankind transformed

This week we will continue exploring the effects of what theologians call the fall. Later we will look at the last two of those aspects—mankind informed and transformed—but this week I want to probe the disruptive and invasive deformation that took place in the lives of the first human pair, Adam and Eve.

The essence of the fall was independent action. The words we heard at the conclusion of the last session are full of sadness and pathos: "He drove the man out" (Gen 3:24).

Both Adam and Eve by their own decision separated themselves from God. Having violated the command of God not to eat of the fruit of the tree of knowledge of good and evil, they were expelled from the garden and its benefits. However, it must be noted that they still retained the image of God in their personalities. The act of sin had defaced that image, of course, but essentially it was still there. They could still think, feel, choose, and relate to one another, albeit not as effectively as they did prior to the fall. In fact, Adam and Eve's sin resulted in the depravity of the whole human race. They were indeed magnificent ruins.

Genesis 5:1-3 records Adam's lineage. "When God created man, he made him in the likeness of God. He created them male and female and blessed them. And when they were created, he called them 'man.' When Adam had lived 130 years, he had a son in his own likeness, in his own image; and he named him Seth."

Note the words again: "When God created man, he made him in the likeness of God" (v. 1). That's how God made Adam, in His own likeness. But then we read "When Adam had lived 130 years, he had a son in his own likeness" (v. 3). Adam and Eve created Seth in their likeness. The depravity that was inside them because of their original sin worked itself out into the next and all subsequent generations. The malignant results of the fall spread throughout the whole human race.

How old does a baby have to be to be termed a sinner?
Explain your answer.

_____

_____

The Bible goes to great lengths to show us that we have inherited from Adam a nature which has a bias toward evil. Some theologians have likened human depravity to a congenital disease. The predisposition is there from earliest infancy. It is infectious; no quarantine can effectively prescribe or limit its incidence. It is disfiguring; it destroys the image so that God cannot see His reflection in us.

Let's focus more closely on the effects of Adam and Eve's sin on our personalities. I want us to see how cataclysmic and pervasive was the damage to them and, as a result, to us. What were the effects of their sin on the relational, rational, emotional, volitional, and physical aspects of our being?

The Relational Damage

Perhaps the very first thing we ought to recognize when thinking of the personality is that we are built for relationships. God is a relational being; so are we. The Almighty has assembled us in such a way that we can only function effectively when we are in relationship—first with Him and then with others. "To be," someone has said, "is to be in relationships." In other words, we don't know who we are unless we experience relationships.

Relationship Between God and Ourselves

Here's the important truth we have to understand—God has built into us a desire for relationship with Him which, if not satisfied, leaves us open and vulnerable to other sources of satisfaction. If God is not satisfying our souls, we will seek something else to satisfy us. Therein lies the truth as to how our personal problems begin.

This yearning for relationship with God is described in the Bible by many words—*desire, hunger, thirst, longings*—but perhaps the most descriptive of these is the word *thirst*. The Bible often uses this word to describe the desire God has given us for Himself.

List the symptoms of a thirst for God. Circle the symptoms you have at present.

1. _____ 2. _____

3. _____ 4. _____

5. _____ 6. _____

Our hearts thirst for something that nothing on earth can satisfy. Most people sense this, but they will not admit it. We have a longing in our souls, a thirst for a relationship with the Creator who formed us in His own image. This yearning is powerful. Even though the yearning may be hidden, ignored, overlaid, and even denied, it has a powerful pull on our personalities.

We can't have a clear sense of our own identity—who we really are—outside of a relationship with God. We don't know *who* we are until we know *whose* we are. To paraphrase the famous words of Augustine, we were made by God and for God, and our identity will never be fully understood and complete until we relate to God.

If God is not satisfying our souls, we will seek something else to satisfy us.

We don't know who we are until we know whose we are.

Between Others and Ourselves

Reflect on how Adam and Eve must have felt there in the garden after the fall. They were together but alone. They had lived together in perfect relationship—no fears, nothing concealed, no suspicions—each enjoying what the other had to give. Now they found themselves in an imperfect relationship beset by fear, suspicion, and terror.

Having shown themselves to be unsure of God, now they were unsure of each other. They were made to connect with God and with each other in perfect harmony, each trusting and caring for the other; but now all that was missing.

Once they doubted the divine love and took the forbidden fruit, the doubt they had of God's love began to show itself in their relationship to each other. They remained alive with a desire and a capacity for love but were left disconnected from God and from each other.

How do you try to cope with relational problems? (underline)

Build walls of denial	Manipulate others
Protect self	Distrust
Relate superficially	Depend on no one
Determine to survive	Other? _____

If it is true that a fundamental terror lies beneath all our relational problems, the root of that terror is the fear that no one will relate to us in the way our hearts desire. We can then easily understand how Adam and Eve sought to insulate themselves from that terror by building walls of denial and superficiality.

Not only did they have terror in their hearts, but also they determined not to trust. Probably nothing fuels determination like terror and lack of trust. They were determined to make their lives work without having to depend on God.

Instead of turning to God and confessing that they had sinned, they arranged for their own survival by trusting in their own human resources. When they discovered they were naked, they covered themselves. The root sinfulness behind that determination was their ongoing suspicion that God was not good enough to be trusted with their lives.

After the fall, Adam and Eve were not only fearful but also deeply determined to survive. They were fueled by the suspicion that neither God nor their mates could provide relief to cope with the terror of disrupted relationships. The fall was not only a physical disaster, but it was also a relational disaster.

The Basis of Identity

I believe our identity as persons depends on three things—a sense that one is unconditionally loved, a sense of one's value as a person, and a sense of meaning and purpose. These three elements can be described by the alliterative words *security, self-worth,* and *significance.* Since these words can mean different things, let me define exactly how I am using them.

1. Security

By *security* I mean the positive feelings that flood the soul when we know we are unconditionally loved. Everyone longs to be loved. We long for love in the present, but each of us also longs to know that love will never ever be taken away. The more we sense that we are loved, the more secure we will feel as persons.

2. Self-Worth

In order to feel at home the soul needs a sense of self-worth. By self-worth I mean a sense of being valued. At first it may seem that the distinction between being loved and being valued is a distinction without a difference. Think of it like this: when we feel loved, we have a sense of being cherished that makes us feel secure; but when we sense that the one who loves us also values us highly, that creates within us a sense of self-worth.

One of the statements I learned when studying adolescent psychology was this: "I am not what I think I am; I am not what you think I am; I am what I think you think I am." A child comes to sense how much he or she is valued not by what the parents (or those responsible for nurture) think but by what the child thinks the parents think of the child. The self is a series of reflected appraisals. We come to think about ourselves in the way we think others think of us. We value ourselves as we think we are valued.

"I am not what I think I am; I am not what you think I am; I am what I think you think I am."

3. Significance

Another quality the soul needs to feel is significance. By this I mean a sense of meaning and purpose. Every person on earth has a divine purpose. No one has a purposeless existence, but we can only realize that purpose as we relate to God and hear Him say: " 'I know the plans I have for you,' declares the Lord, 'plans to prosper you and not to harm you, plans to give you hope and a future. Then you will call upon me and come and pray to me, and I will listen to you. You will seek me and find me when you seek me with all your heart' " (Jer. 29:11-13).

> **Label the following as possible problems relating to SC (security), SW (self-worth), or SF (significance).**
> ___ Janet didn't want to practice the piano. "Don't you know mommy loves seeing you on that piano bench?" her mother chided.
> ___ Yes, her father had wanted a son to leave in charge of the company, but Emily was working hard to learn the business.
> ___ Because his father was in the military and away a lot, Paul kept trying to earn his dad's approval.

Now with those three words in mind—security, self-worth, and significance—come back with me once more to the story of Adam and Eve in their sinless state in the garden of Eden. Picture them standing on a firm and steady three-legged stool. Now let's give names to each one of those legs—security, self-worth, and significance. Because of their close relationship with God, Adam and Eve knew what it meant to be unconditionally loved, highly valued, and purposeful.

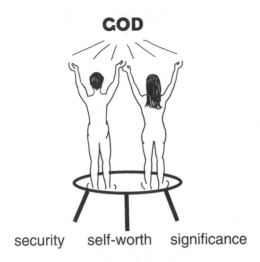

GOD

security   self-worth   significance

When their relationship with God was severed by their act of sin, however, it was as if the legs of the stool were broken and their security became insecurity, their self-worth reverted to inferiority, and their significance turned into insignificance. Thus took place the world's first identity crisis.

GOD

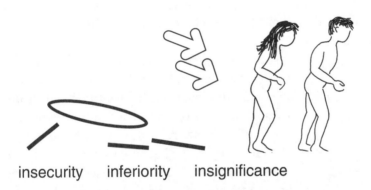

insecurity   inferiority   insignificance

Since Adam and Eve's fall, everyone born into this world arrives with a soul that carries within it a deep sense of insecurity, inferiority, and insignificance. No human love can give us what our souls long for. Bereft of a relationship with God, the best that earthly relationships (such as parents, friends, and peers) can do is to make us feel only moderately secure, worthwhile, and significant. People are not enough. Our best friends are not enough.

Only God can meet the longings deep within us. We will never resolve the identity crisis in our souls until we know how to relate to the true God who alone can give us what our souls require: unconditional love, value, and eternal meaning.

In fact, we are all longing to get back to what was lost by our first parents in the garden of Eden. These longings are the most powerful part of our personalities. Our longings fuel our search for meaning, for wholeness, for a sense of being truly alive. They are the most important things about us, and the voice that calls us is the voice of God.

Our longings fuel our search for meaning, for wholeness, for a sense of being truly alive.

Fill in the blanks with your personal testimony.

1. I feel loved when _____

2. I believe I am valued when _____

3. I think my life has purpose when _____

Unsatisfied Deep Longings

This thirst in our souls, if not satisfied in God, lies behind most of the problems of the personality. Take almost any psychological problem you can name. When you cut through all the labels psychologists give to these various conditions, you come to a person who is not experiencing deeply enough what it means to be loved and valued and to have a sense of purpose. Problems arise when we try to meet these three deepest needs of the soul outside of God. When these deep needs are not met, to that degree we will experience problems.

Seeking to meet these needs outside of God steers us in the wrong direction, and obsessions and compulsions occur. We will turn easily to other sources of satisfaction. Things such as masturbation, pornography, and overeating have a tremendous appeal for us when our spirits lack the life and joy that come from a relationship with God through His Son Jesus Christ.

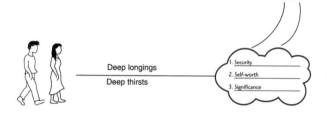

If you want a key to understanding how problems arise in the personality, it lies in unsatisfied deep longings. God designed our beings for the most incredible joy and satisfaction, but if we do not experience a close and intimate relationship with the Father, Son, and Holy Spirit, we become extremely vulnerable to those things that excite our senses and explode with passion temporarily. We find ourselves living for them or depending on them to bring a sense of aliveness to our souls.

How Problems Arise

1. Unsatisfied deep longings

Let me summarize what I have said before moving on to look at the damage sin has caused to another aspect of our personalities. As a result of the fall that took place in the garden of Eden, we come into this world with souls that do not naturally relate to God. Yet, because the soul was made by God and for God, the soul cannot be fully satisfied until it relates to Him. This is the great human predicament.

We long for God, we want God, but sin in our system causes us to stay independent of Him. So we try to find satisfaction in some other source. We can't, but we want to because embedded like splintered glass deep within our souls is a stubborn commitment to independence. Adam and Eve's act of independence.has been repeated by everyone on earth.

Based on what you have just read in the last paragraph, number 1 through 4 the sin cycle that leads to unsatisfied deep longings.

___ We seek satisfaction some other way.
___ We long for God.
___ We can't find satisfaction.
___ Sin keeps us away from God.

THE RATIONAL DAMAGE

We are more than just relational beings whose deep thirst and longings remain unsatisfied unless we are in a relationship with God. We are also rational beings who can think. Consider now how Adam and Eve's minds were affected by the fall. Whereas before they had a clear understanding of God, now their minds were darkened.

Prior to the fall, Adam and Eve were able to think clearly and accurately about everything. They understood the things of God—His purpose in creating them, their ability to do God's work and will, and the perpetuation of the glory of God through the human race. They chose to act in ways that were in harmony with the divine will. Enlightened intelligence kindled perfect emotions. Seeing God clearly, they loved Him intensely and served Him wholly.

Recall the process of temptation. When one doubts God, the whole personality capitulates. Doubt is like a termite that brings down the house. Adam and Eve entertained doubt about God's goodness. Doubt led to disliking God and ultimately to disobedience.

This ache we feel in our hearts for a relationship with God is not something God condemns. However, what He does condemn is the pointless ways we go about trying to find satisfaction for that ache in ways other than Him. The foolish directions we follow to find a way of gaining security, self-worth, and significance have their origins in the mind.

Our minds have been enemy territory ever since Adam and Eve allowed Satan to violate their personalities. The devil succeeded in establishing a bridgehead in our minds and continuously sends his envoys across it to militate against the influences of the Trinity.

Read the first three Scriptures in the margin. What was Satan's point of attack on these persons/groups?

"They exchanged the truth of God for a lie, and worshiped and served created things rather than the Creator—who is forever praised."
—ROMANS 1:25

Not everyone is willing to admit that the mind is one of Satan's strongholds. "What's wrong with my mind?" people will say. "I am a perfectly normal and rational person." But a world of difference exists between what the world accepts as normal and what Scripture teaches is normal. The world accepts as normal such things as outbursts of temper, occasional white lies, living together outside of marriage, and taking care of number one. The New Testament tells us that by claiming the power that comes from Jesus Christ we can live above all these wrong behaviors—and live without strain.

The Essence of the Lie

An interesting verse in Paul's epistle to the Romans reads: "They exchanged the truth of God for a lie, and worshiped and served created things rather than the Creator—who is forever praised" (1:25).

What was the essence of the lie that the first human pair exchanged for the truth? First let's understand what truth filled their minds in the days prior to their fall. The truth was this—by remaining dependent on God for their life and obeying His command not to eat of the fruit of the tree of knowledge of good and evil, they would experience perfect joy and happiness. Satan's lie was just the opposite. The essence of that lie was this—you can be a more fulfilled person by acting independently of God. By exchanging that lie for the truth, they plunged each of their descendants into moral darkness.

We now have a blindness in our minds. Though it does not prevent us from understanding many of the wonderful things about the universe, it stops us from seeing the truth that life, true life, is found only in following the design of God for our lives.

The Bible uses a very interesting word to describe this mental blackout—our inability to figure out what life is all about. It is called *folly* or *foolishness*. The Book of Proverbs has a good deal to say about this.

Read the three Proverbs passages in the margin. Write *T* (true) or *F* (false) for each statement.
___ A fool thinks his way is right.
___ A fool hesitates to say what he thinks.
___ Discipline drives folly from the heart of a child.

A fool in the Book of Proverbs is not someone who is, as we say, intellectually challenged. A fool is someone who thinks he knows where life is to be found but doesn't.

Each of us comes into the world with the foolish idea that life can be found through our own resources and our own efforts. God says it can't. We think we know better.

This truth is very important. What is the most foolish thing we can believe?

_____

This mental strategy to bypass God in our efforts to satisfy our souls' deepest longings and thirsts is brought out most clearly by the prophet Jeremiah:

*"My people have committed two sins:
They have forsaken me,*

> the spring of living water,
>   and have dug their own cisterns,
>   broken cisterns that cannot hold water" (Jer. 2:13).

If you read the context you discover that a trial is in progress. God is charging His people with foolishly trying to find life outside of their relationship with Him. Speaking metaphorically, He accuses them of preferring to dig their own broken cisterns rather than rely in humble dependence on the Lord and turn to Him for flowing springs of water.

How pained God sounds as He observes His people spurning His offer of living water which was free for the taking and instead laboriously digging their own cisterns. It is utter foolishness. Why would people walk past a fountain of fresh water and go out into the desert to dig wells to find water that is dirty, bacteria infected, lukewarm, and soon leaks away. It doesn't make any sense unless you understand that our minds have been affected and infected by the lie that Adam and Eve fell for, namely that we can be more fulfilled by acting independently of God.

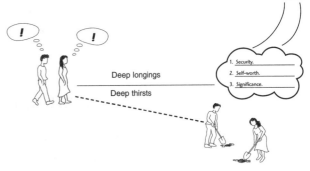

Sin has so affected our minds that we foolishly believe we can satisfy through our own devices the ache in our souls. We can't, but we prefer to believe that we can, and that thought is reinforced by the commitment to independence that lies deep within our souls.

Something in each of us hates the fact that apart from God we will never be able to satisfy the deep thirst of our souls. Facing that truth requires that we adopt a position of helplessness—giving up our vain attempts to make life work without God. Helplessness, that feeling we can't make it on our own, is something our carnal nature abhors. We much prefer to be in control of the water we drink. It feels good to be in control, much better than feeling helpless, but the Bible regards that strategy as foolishness.

Unnoticed Wrong Thinking

Unsatisfied deep longing was the first reason for what is wrong with our souls. But we are not just thirsty, we are beings who can think, and we foolishly believe that we can quench our thirst through some other route than God, by drinking from cisterns of our own making. These cisterns, however, do not hold satisfying water. They also leak. So we go from one broken cistern to another, driven by foolish strategies that make us feel we are in control. How foolish. Sin has made us believers, not in God, but in ourselves. **The second key, then, to understanding how problems arise in our souls is—unnoticed wrong thinking.**

Once Adam and Eve were distanced from God, they developed strategies in their minds to bolster their confidence so their lives could work without God. One strategy was blaming others for their own failure.

We have already seen how this works when Adam blamed his wife and his wife blamed the serpent. Blame is often a way the soul protects itself

How Problems Arise

1. Unsatisfied deep longings
2. Unnoticed wrong thinking

against terror. In the context of feeling terror, a terror fueled by the determination to survive without having to depend on God, their beliefs would have solidified. One wonders how long they endured with that doubt of God and doubt of each other in their hearts.

Clearly the fall was a rational disaster also.

Do you struggle with the temptation to blame others for what went wrong? ❏ Yes ❏ No
Do you agree that blaming is often a way we choose to bolster our self-confidence? ❏ Yes ❏ No
Pause to say a prayer asking for God's help to break this sin cycle.

Learning from the Mistakes of Others

Last week we learned that King Saul had an impressive physical appearance but not a strong self-image. In fact, when he was to be presented at his coronation, he hid among the baggage! The story continues.

Relational Issues

Our relationship to God is the key to experiencing true security, self-worth, and significance. Without a doubt, Saul knew *about* God but how well did he *know* God? He may have had a formal relationship with Him, in the sense that he prayed and participated in the religious ceremonies and rituals of Israel, but the question that needs to be asked is: how deep was that relationship?

Recall from your reading of 1 Samuel 9 that it was the servant's persistence that encouraged Saul to continue the search for the man of God (v. 8). Then when Saul found him, Samuel prophesied great blessings on his father's family. Saul could not believe his words.

> *Saul answered, "But am I not a Benjamite, from the smallest tribe of Israel, and is not my clan the least of all the clans of the tribe of Benjamin? Why do you say such a thing to me?" (1 Sam. 9:21).*

The deeper a person's relationship with God, the greater resources he or she has to function in the way God designed—with a strong sense of inner confidence and intactness. The fact that Saul lacked this confidence indicates that he was basing his identity on the world's value system: coming from a large family with a lot of wealth and status.

The fact that at the moment of his coronation Saul could not be found because he was hiding among the baggage would suggest that he was a reluctant king. Saul lacked a deep relationship with the Almighty who had selected him.

Rational Issues

Having seen the lack in Saul's relationship with God, we must look now at the rational areas of King Saul's functioning.

One incident in 1 Samuel 15:12 puts a clear focus on his wrong thinking. "Early in the morning Samuel got up and went to meet Saul, but he was told, 'Saul has gone to Carmel. There he has set up a monument in his own honor and has turned and gone on down to Gilgal.' "

Remember the theory once again; whatever we believe will bring us security, self-worth, and significance will become our goal. Here we have additional information as to Saul's wrong beliefs, which fuelled the pursuit of his goal—the commendation and applause of the people.

If we could have tape recorded King Saul's deepest and most honest thoughts, perhaps even below the level of consciousness, as he set about building a monument to himself, what do you think we might have heard? It may have sounded something like this: "If I am to experience inward satisfaction and intactness, then I must impress the people. Their opinion of me is vital to my self-worth and maintaining my support. I will put up a monument to myself so that the people will have a constant reminder of how great I am. I don't feel very great on the inside, so perhaps doing something like this on the outside might help me feel more secure and significant."

This, of course, is foolish thinking which leads to drinking at a leaky well. Many other evidences of King Saul's wrong thinking—thinking which fuelled his goal of gaining the admiration and commendation of the people—can be identified in Scripture.

Identify the evidence of King Saul's wrong thinking as you read 1 Samuel 13:1-15.

_____

_____

_____

Next week we will consider some additional evidences of Saul's questionable behavior.

---

[1]Dr. Larry Crabb, *Who We Are and How We Relate* (Colorado Springs: NavPress, 1992), 29-30.

Session 4: Depravity: Deeper Than You Think

We have examined what sin has done to the relational and rational aspects of our personalities. However, there is more to us than the capacities we have looked at so far.

Human beings were designed not only to relate and think but also to _____.

1. Behind any unit of behavior lies a _____.

2. A powerful insight into the personality is that all behavior moves towards a

   _____.

3. Scripture tells us in _____ that behind all behavior is a plan.

4. The third reason why problems arise in the personality is due to

   _____ _____ _____.

Another aspect of human functioning is the fact that we have emotions. We can _____.

5. The first negative emotion that we see in Scripture is _____.

6. Negative emotions most often arise from a failure to reach a _____

   we believe we must reach in order to feel good about ourselves.

7. Consider the concept of _____ _____ which act like the red

   warning lights on the dashboards of our cars.

8. Unpleasant or problem emotions can be categorized into three main streams:

   a. Feelings that come from a goal that is undermined or blocked—

      _____ and _____.

b. Feelings that come from pursuing a goal that is uncertain—_____

and _____.

c. Feelings that come from pursuing a goal that is unreachable—_____

and _____.

9. The fourth reason why we have problems in our personality is due to

_____ _____ _____.

A final aspect of human functioning that has to be considered is the fact that we are _____ _____.

10. Before Adam and Eve were created, a complete support system was provided:

_____, _____, _____.

11. Due to the fall, no human body functions in the way it was _____.

12. The _____ and the _____ are so intertwined that what goes wrong

in one area can affect the other.

13. Some problems which may appear to be spiritual may be rooted in a

malfunctioning _____.

14. The fifth and final reason why we have problems may be traced to

_____ _____ _____.

Week Four
DEPRAVITY: DEEPER THAN YOU THINK

*"The Lord saw how great man's wickedness on the earth
had become, and that every inclination of the thoughts
of his heart was only evil all the time."*

GENESIS 6:5

Scripture teaches that when Adam fell, he fell all the way. He became so depraved that he could do nothing to save himself or those who came after him. And those who came after him were as depraved as he.

The first human beings made such a mess of things that God decided to start again. Only eight people survived the great Flood. Would a new start make a difference? Sadly, no. When we step out of Genesis 7 into the later chapters of this first book of the Bible, we find the same things occurring all over again—murder, lust, sin, and rebellion.

In Genesis 19, we have the story of another environmental disaster, when once again God was so tired of rampant sin in the twin cities of Sodom and Gomorrha that he decided to destroy all the inhabitants.

Clearly the human race was infected and affected with a disease far more dangerous than cancer or heart disease. Theologians call it "depravity." What exactly is depravity? The dictionary says that depravity is "the innate moral corruption of human nature."

A more theological definition of *depravity* is this: the desire to make our lives work independently of God. We don't like God telling us what to do. All of us carry this propensity within us. One of the most powerful statements that shows us the extent of depravity can be seen by a glance at Genesis 6:5. Read it again at the top of the page.

Note the words "every inclination of the thoughts of his heart was only evil all the time." Not *occasionally* but *perpetually*. Every person on the face of planet Earth is a depraved human being. The scars of sin are never hidden.

As you read, keep these questions in mind:
1. Is behavior chosen or a matter of instinct?
2. What are five keys to problems that arise in the personality?
3. What are three main streams of problem emotions?

In the previous session we looked at the damage Adam and Eve's sin has done to the relational and rational parts of our personalities. We are all thirsty for a relationship with God, and only as we relate to Him can we find true satisfaction for our souls. But we are not only thirsty; we are also foolish. We believe that we can find satisfaction for our souls through our own foolish strategies, and we pursue these ways because we like to feel we are in control.

The Volitional Damage

We are not only relational and rational beings but also volitional beings. We can choose. That is the ability God gave to the first human pair, Adam and Eve, and that ability remains within us as part of God's image.

The fact that the Creator has endowed us with the ability to choose and go against His will if we prefer is perhaps one of the most amazing aspects of our construction as human beings. God allows us to exercise our own wills even though our choices may collide with His. How awesome that God would create a will that has the potential of competing with His own. That thought is some measure of the respect God has for His creation.

Behind All Behavior Lies a Choice

Behind any unit of behavior lies a choice. Formerly I thought that some occasions in our lives—such as when we react in anger toward someone who has hurt us—were a matter of instinct. I came to see, however, that we choose to become angry even though we do not feel as if we are choosing.

Why do extremely shy persons experience their shyness as something that is part of their makeup rather than something they are choosing? Behind the shyness lies choice—the choice to avoid people because of the threat that close relationships may surface a fear of being unable to relate. Safety lies in hiding.

If you want to think more deeply about this, consider an area of your life over which you feel you have no control (such as anger, overeating, an undisciplined tongue). Try and ponder whether it is choosing you or you are choosing it. Sin has so damaged our personalities that in many ways we have lost the awareness of choice. Often when we choose we don't realize we are choosing.

Take the challenge. Select a negative behavior in your life over which you feel you have little control. List one or more reasons why you may be choosing this behavior.

_____

_____

"The loss of felt choice
does not mean the loss
of real choice."

My friend Larry Crabb has a powerful phrase that illustrates this concept of unrealized choices. He says that "the loss of felt choice does not mean the loss of real choice."[1] Often we may feel driven by internal dynamics, driven against our will. The truth is that we choose to behave the way we do, even though sometimes the choice may only take a split second.

A friend of mine was taken to court by his neighbor because of an altercation. The neighbor said something derogatory about my friend's wife, and my friend punched the neighbor on the nose. Prior to the court proceedings, he approached me to see if I would be a character witness for him. I asked him how he planned to plead before the court.

This was his reply: "I will say, 'I had to hit him.' He cast aspersions on my wife … it was an instinctive reaction." I suggested that he did not have to hit him; he chose to hit him. He came to see that it was a bad defense to hide behind instinct and apologized to his neighbor. The case was eventually dropped. We may lose a subjective awareness that what we do is the result of a choice, but, nevertheless, what we do is what we choose to do.

All Behavior Moves Toward a Goal

Not only is all behavior a choice, but all behavior moves toward a goal. Psychologist Alfred Adler said that when examining any unit of behavior, it may be more useful not to look so much to the past (though sometimes that is important) but to ask yourself: what is the goal to which the behavior is being directed?[2]

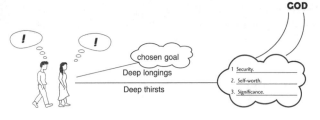

During the early years of my counseling ministry, I spent a great deal of time digging into people's pasts to find an explanation for their behavior. Though sometimes that is important, we can learn a lot more about why we behave the way we do by looking at the goal to which the behavior is being directed. Even the most bizarre behavior makes sense when we understand the underlying goal.

What is the goal behind a young girl's becoming involved in the pursuit of thinness—anorexia nervosa? Most likely it is control. A young girl who may feel somewhat stifled in her personal life or controlled by others can easily develop this condition. Through it she may gain a sense of being in control of part of her life even though she may feel controlled in other parts.

Read Proverbs 19:21 in the margin. Behind all behavior is a plan. We behave in ways that bring us rewards. Everything we do represents an effort we make to reach a goal even at an unconscious level.

"Many are the plans in
a man's heart,
but it is the LORD's
purpose that prevails."
—PROVERBS 19.21

Draw a line to match the probable cause with the following behaviors?

A person talks all the time.	To get you to like him or her
A person is overly friendly.	To protect themselves
A person is overly shy.	To be in control

Whatever we believe will bring satisfaction to our souls quickly becomes our goal. If a man believes that money is the route to happiness, then what will be his goal? Get money. If a woman believes that getting her husband's attention is what will bring her security, what will be her goal? Getting her husband's attention. Finding the goal to which the behavior is directed can be a most illuminating exercise. It helps us understand why we do what we do.

Identify the probable goal behind each of these behaviors.

Habitually arrives late _____

Wears message tee shirts _____

Routinely exceeds speed limits _____

Piles up credit card debt _____

Consider where we are now in our examination of the depravity that has affected the different parts of our personalities. We have a heart that aches for something that nothing in this world can satisfy. We have a mind that foolishly believes our deep longings and deep thirsts can be satisfied by pursuing ways to get satisfaction other than God. With the pain of our unmet longings and thirsts driving us to find relief and with the foolish idea that they can be met apart from a relationship with God, we pursue goals we believe will bring us the satisfaction our heart craves.

As a result of the depravity caused by Adam and Eve's sin, **unrecognized wrong goals are the next key to understanding how problems arise in the personality.**

HOW PROBLEMS ARISE

1. Unsatisfied deep longings
2. Unnoticed wrong thinking
3. Unrecognized wrong goals

Ruined Choices

The will desires mastery. Strong-willed people want their own way. They want the wills of others to bend to them. They get their kicks this way. This behavior can lead to tyranny. God's will intends others' well-being, not mastery over them.

The doctrine of the freedom of the will is itself true only within certain limitations. We cannot will that night be day or that up be down. In a sense, the very nature of the will cannot be free.

Humankind constantly asserts, "I will." The full statement, however, must always be, "I will because ..." That which follows the "because" is the authority behind the will, the power that commands it. Man never wills except under the impulse of a conviction. Behind every action of the will must be a governing principle.

To us it seems humorous when a small child stomps his feet and says "I will" or "I won't" with no power to command it. Have you said to God, "I will" or "I won't," rejecting His authority over your life? If so, pause now and confess this sin.

Although we will because of some reason that may or may not be apparent, the same is not true of God. A wonderful passage in the Book of

Deuteronomy shows that there is no reason (as we understand it) behind God's love. God doesn't need a reason to love. He loves because He is love.

Moses said, "The LORD did not set his affection on you and choose you because you were more numerous than other peoples, for you were the fewest of all peoples. But it was because the LORD loved you and kept the oath he swore to your forefathers that he brought you out with a mighty hand and redeemed you from the land of slavery, from the power of Pharaoh king of Egypt" (Deut. 7:7-8).

Explain how giving humans volitional choice was a loving deed on God's part.

_____

_____

Thus in the garden of His activity, God marked the limits of humankind's possibility by two sacramental symbols—both trees. One was the tree of life from which they could eat; the other, the tree of the knowledge of good and evil from which they were not to eat. The tree of life reminded Adam and Eve of their dependence on God for the sustenance of their life. Their wills were under test. They were sovereigns under Sovereignty. Independent yet dependent. Sadly, they failed the test.

The will cannot succeed in its attempt to secure mastership outside of God. People ask, "Why is it that I don't have much willpower?" Because of the fall, human will nevers function effectively unless it corresponds with the divine will. Tennyson put it like this:

> Our wills are ours, we know not how
> Our wills are ours to make them thine.[3]

The Emotional Damage

We need to consider another area of the personality to complete our understanding of the degree of damage done to God's image in us as a result of the fall. Adam and Eve's sinful behavior resulted in damage to our emotional makeup.

God made us in the beginning to enjoy and experience positive emotions such as love, joy, happiness, pleasure, and delight. Negative emotions such as fear, anger, and hostility did not exist prior to the fall. As soon as Adam and Eve sinned, negative emotions began to arise in their hearts. God came looking for them following their act of transgression: "Then the man and his wife heard the sound of the LORD God as he was walking in the garden in the cool of the day, and they hid from the LORD God among the trees of the garden. But the LORD God called to the man, 'Where are you?' He answered, 'I heard you in the garden, and I was afraid because I was naked; so I hid' " (Gen. 3:8-10).

The very first negative emotion we come across in Scripture is fear. Other negative emotions such as shame are revealed in their desire to cover up their nakedness. Blame-shifting, an attempt on Adam's part to avoid guilt by projecting it on to his wife, began its long history. "The man said, 'The woman you put here with me—she gave me some fruit from the tree, and I ate it' " (Gen. 3:12).

The very first negative emotion we come across in Scripture is fear.

Source of Negative Emotions

Many different theories exist as to how negative emotions arise within the personality. The most helpful theory I have come across is the one that says negative emotions most often arise from a failure to reach a goal which we believe we must reach in order to feel good about ourselves.

Prior to the fall, Adam and Eve had only one clear goal in their life—to love and obey God. As long as they pursued that goal, their relationship with God and with each other was one of happiness and joy. They fulfilled the command God later gave to all people.

Every emotion felt by Adam and Eve prior to their sin in the garden was in harmony with that command. They loved God, and they loved each other. Once they sinned, however, their emotions reflected the operation of sin in their minds. Now their minds contained thoughts of distrust and suspicion toward God. Soon it affected the way they felt about Him.

When they pursued the goal of attempting to become more fulfilled persons by acting independently of God, they brought about a disorder in their makeup that affected not only them but every one of their descendants. Because of this disorder, we can usually trace the negative emotions in our lives to experiencing an obstacle on the road to a foolish or unbiblical goal.

Trace a negative emotion you often feel (such as anger, fear, shame) when your progress toward a goal you are trying to achieve is threatened. For example, you may want a promotion (goal) but when Shawn gets it (obstacle), you feel jealous (emotion). You note that you often feel jealousy toward others. Now you try it.

_____	_____	_____
(Goal)	− (Obstacle)	= (Emotion)

Think of emotions like the red light on a car's dashboard. The red light is not the problem, but it indicates a problem that needs attention. I like the way Kevin Huggins puts it in *Parenting Adolescents:* "God has given each of us a 'warning system' to alert us when we are pursuing a foolish goal. This system consists of a series of *signal emotions* that reliably indicate the nature of the goal we are pursuing at any given moment."[4]

Huggins calls negative feelings "signal emotions" because they act like the red lights on the dashboard of our cars telling us that all is not well with our internal emotional system.

Personally, I have found it helpful to categorize unpleasant or problem emotions into three main streams.: **First,** emotions such as anger, irritation, resentment, frustration, and contempt. **Second,** emotions such as fear, anxiety, worry, apprehension, pressure, and different forms of stress. **Third,** emotions such as guilt, shame, embarrassment, and self-pity.

Let's look at how these three streams of emotions relate to a failure to reach a goal which we believe we must reach in order to feel good about ourselves.

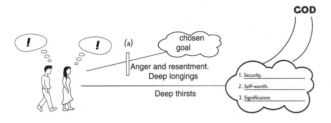

First, feelings such as anger, irritation, resentment, and contempt arise when a goal we are pursuing becomes blocked by an external circumstance. For example, if my goal in life is to make money and someone or something blocks my goal, then the usual reaction is to feel irritation or anger. The degree of the emotion will depend on the degree of importance I attach to reaching my goal. If I am only moderately dependent on money as the route to feeling good about myself, I will feel only a moderate degree of negative emotions. If I am strongly dependent on money to form my identity as a person, I will feel the negative emotions more strongly.

I think James in his epistle put this thought into clear focus. Read James 4:1-2 in the margin.

What does James say is the source of fights and quarrels?

_____

What happens when the goal is not attained?

_____

What is a godly way to reach a godly goal?

_____

> *"What causes fights and quarrels among you? Don't they come from your desires that battle within you? You want something but don't get it. You kill and covet, but you cannot have what you want. You quarrel and fight. You do not have, because you do not ask God."*
>
> —James 4:1-2

When we pursue unbiblical goals, any block to those goals can arouse emotions within us that can become, in their extreme form, a danger to our emotional and even our physical health. Feelings such as fear, anxiety, worry, and pressure indicate that we may be pursuing a goal whose attainment is uncertain. These feelings may signal that we are putting our trust in something or someone for fulfillment, but we are unsure that the objective will be realized.

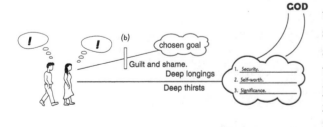

The third stream of problem emotions are those that arise from pursuing an unattainable goal. Guilt, shame, and self-pity are some of the emotions that appear in this category. When we hold within ourselves the perception that attaining a certain goal carries the promise that our life is to be found there, failure to reach it can result in feelings such as guilt and shame. Some goals we set are unattainable, no matter how hard we try.

A missionary I worked with told me that she was continually plagued with feelings of guilt and shame even though she was not involved in any moral violations. During counseling, we discovered that she strongly believed that she must do everything perfectly. "Every night," she said, "I make a list of the things I have to do the next day; and if I am not able to do them all, I go to my bed with great feelings of guilt and shame."

This woman's objective was the unattainable goal of perfection. Whenever she failed to achieve her goal, she came down hard on herself. Her problem resolved when she understood that good feelings about herself did not depend on doing everything perfectly but rather on how well she related to God and His evaluation of her worth.

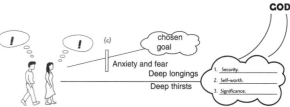

The fourth reason why problems arise in the personality is because of unsettling negative emotions. Underlying all negative emotions is self-centeredness and self-interest. All negative emotions arise because of the absence of love. Where love is not, other emotions flow through the personality. One of the reasons we call them negative emotions is because they oppose the design of the personality. They are all anti-love. Where love is, fear is not. Where love is, anger is not. Where love is, guilt is not.

Write the name of several safe people with whom you can share your flaws and mistakes, and they won't shame you.

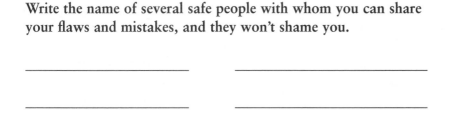

If you don't have such friends, you would be right to pray for such a friend. However, pray to be such a friend for someone else.

How Problems Arise

1. Unsatisfied deep longings
2. Unnoticed wrong thinking
3. Unrecognized wrong goals
4. Unsettling negative emotions

Self-Centered Love

Adam and Eve's emotional makeup was at one time like God's, but after the fall it became unlike God. Lacking the driving force of true love, their emotions became selfish. Instead of self-love they had become lovers of themselves.

God loves in the very necessity of His being and in such a way as to make the thought of selfishness forever impossible. On the other hand, our deepest emotions tend to move toward the gratification of desires. We love those who love us. Love can rise to high levels, but basically love of self is selfish and filled with self-centered interests.

God's love is spiritual, self-sacrificing, and set upon objects utterly unworthy of His love— those who have given Him no reason to love them. The love Adam and Eve had was self-love that had turned to love of self. Thus, the emotions of Adam and Eve were depraved. How different this was from the love of God that had shaped their personalities prior to the fall.

Label these people as showing L (love of self) or S (self-love).
___ Karen runs at least a mile a day to keep physically fit.
___ Andrea left the choir loft to check her makeup before her special music.
___ Teri knew her clothes were more stylish than anyone else's at the party.
___ Lyle was pleased with his score on the final exam.

The Physical Damage

" 'Love the Lord your God with all your heart and with all your soul and with all your mind and with all your strength.' The second is this: 'Love your neighbor as yourself.' There is no commandment greater than these."
—MARK 12:30-31

We have one more area of our being to explore—the physical. When God designed us, He placed the image of Himself within a physical frame—a body. Look at this text once again: "The Lord God formed the man from the dust of the ground and breathed into his nostrils the breath of life, and the man became a living being" (Gen. 2:7).

Adam was created a physical being. He was made from the dust of the earth. There isn't a chemical in our bodies that cannot be found in the Scripture: "All go to the same place; all come from dust, and to dust all return" (Eccl. 3:20). Before Adam and Eve were created, a complete support system was brought into being for them: air to breathe, water to drink, food to eat. Adam was made from the dust of the earth and Eve from Adam's side, so both were physical beings.

After they had sinned, however, their bodies were greatly affected, and the legacy they left us is that no human body functions perfectly and in the way it was originally designed. Sickness and afflictions beset us all.

The interesting thing is this—the soul and the body are so intertwined that when the body doesn't function properly, it can affect the functioning of our inner being—our souls. When you bang your thumb, it alters your perception of things for a few moments, doesn't it? Your mind, your worldview, is temporarily influenced by what goes on in your body. The world looks like a different place for a while.

A virus can cause depression; having a baby can produce great mood changes; significant sleep loss can produce hallucinations. Some counselors often forget this connection when they are trying to help people with their problems. If you are dealing with someone who has serious emotional problems, first explore the possibility of some physical difficulty triggering the problem. We live in a material creation, in bodies that have suffered because of Adam and Eve's fall.

Stress has been defined as a person's response to overload. How does your body let you know when it is stressed? (Underline)

Gaining weight	Losing weight	Sleepiness	Constipation
Weak immune system	Headaches	Lack of sleep	Diarrhea
Irregular heartbeat	Backaches	Other _____	

I remember on one occasion a woman came to me with a child she said was demon possessed. Apparently, she had been in church one day and her

4-year-old child had run to the front of the church while a visiting evangelist was preaching and then raced backwards and forwards distracting the preacher who stopped and said: "That child is demon possessed."

As I talked with the child, I sensed no demonic activity. However, the child was obviously hyperactive. I arranged an appointment with a medical doctor who concluded that the child had slight brain damage which was contributing to the hyperactivity. The appropriate medication helped to bring the condition under control. Within a few weeks the child was acting and behaving normally.

Some problems that appear to be emotional or even spiritual may have their roots in a malfunctioning physiology. Throughout the time I have been a counselor and a pastor, I have learned the wisdom of recognizing the interaction between our bodies and souls.

A deacon asked me on one occasion if I could help him with a spiritual problem with which he was struggling. It seemed that whenever he knelt to pray or read the Bible, he would quickly lose interest. Consequently his spiritual life, he said, was being compromised.

Before counseling him, I suggested he have a medical checkup. The doctor discovered that he was suffering from hypoglycemia—low blood sugar. Medication helped to bring the matter under control, and within days his so-called spiritual problem was resolved. The problem was not spiritual but rooted in the physical. His propensity to quickly lose interest came from a chemical imbalance which affected his mental and emotional makeup.

One doctor told me that 120 things can go wrong with our thumbs. One thing is clear: the functioning of our mental and emotional makeup is tied to our physical bodies. We need to understand this fact clearly, especially those of us who are involved in helping people with their problems.

Just as the body affects the soul, so the soul can affect the body. Our doctors have come up with the word, *psychosomatic,* which really consists of two separate words—*psyche* meaning *soul* and *soma* meaning *body.* A disturbance in our soul can affect the body in many ways. Harboring resentment, for example, can produce physical problems.

Good stress is called eustress—that extra rush of adrenaline you may need to complete a task or handle an emergency. Distress often comes from taking on more than God intended. How do you know when an assignment is from God or from a human source?
❏ The nominating committee couldn't find anyone else.
❏ The person enlisting me had prayed about it.
❏ I couldn't think of an excuse.
❏ I knew I would do a good job.
❏ I had prayed and sought God's will.

The fifth and final cause for behavior can be unsound physical functioning. With the advances of modern medicine, many conditions which appeared to be mental or emotional have been successfully treated as a physical malfunctioning of chemical or hormonal imbalance.

HOW PROBLEMS ARISE

1. Unsatisfied deep longings
2. Unnoticed wrong thinking
3. Unrecognized wrong goals
4. Unsettling negative emotions
5. Unsound physical functioning

How do problems arise in our personalities? If the problem is not due to physiological factors, then consider the possibility that it results from trying to meet our basic needs for security, self-worth, and significance elsewhere rather than in God. We then pursue goals which we believe will make us feel more secure, significant, and worthwhile. When these goals are blocked, we experience a variety of emotions, which sometimes become so turbulent and incapacitating that they conflict greatly with the abundant life that Jesus talked about in John 10:10.

Now that we have examined the causes of behavior, how things have gone so wrong in our personalities, how do we go about correcting the faults and flaws? How do we move toward experiencing the inner spiritual peace and power that the New Testament appears to offer us? That's our next focus.

Learning from the Mistakes of Others

Last week we explored the relational and rational damage that occurred as Saul rose to become king of the nation of Israel. This week we will look at the emotional facet of his personality.

Emotional Windows

Emotions are like the red warning lights we have on the car's dashboard letting us know that something is wrong.

Having surmised that Saul lacked a deep relationship with God, consider now what might have been going on in King Saul's emotions. Remember what we said about problem emotions? Emotions are like the red warning lights we have on the car's dashboard letting us know that something is wrong. The most troublesome problem emotions are guilt and shame, fear and anxiety, and anger and resentment. Problem emotions arise due to frustration about reaching a goal which we believe we must reach in order to feel good about ourselves.

Focus on the following texts and see which of the three streams of dominant emotions you think Saul was struggling with: (underline)
Guilt and shame   Fear and anxiety   Anger and resentment

When the men were returning home after David had killed the Philistine, the women came out from all the towns of Israel to meet King Saul with singing and dancing, with joyful songs and with tambourines and lutes. As they danced, they sang:

"Saul has slain his thousands,
  and David his tens of thousands."

Saul was very angry; this refrain galled him. "They have credited David with tens of thousands," he thought, "but me with only thousands. What more can he get but the kingdom?" And from that time on Saul kept a jealous eye on David" (1 Sam. 18:6-9).

Let's take a look through another window and see Saul's emotional spectrum in 1 Samuel 20:25-31. Read this passage in your Bible. David is well aware of Saul's hatred of him and that Saul is bent on his destruction, so he confides in Saul's son Jonathan. David must be absent from a new moon festival. When the king saw that he was absent, he asked where David was. Jonathan tried to speak up for David and became another victim of Saul's wrath.

> *"Saul's anger flared up at at Jonathan and he said to him, 'You son of a perverse and rebellious woman! Don't I know that you have sided with the son of Jesse to your own shame and to the shame of the mother who bore you? As long as the son of Jesse lives on this earth, neither you nor your kingdom will be established. Now send and bring him to me, for he must die!' 'Why should he be put to death? What has he done?' Jonathan asked his father. But Saul hurled his spear at him to kill him. Then Jonathan knew that his father intended to kill David" (1 Sam. 20:30-31).*

Whatever other emotions were going on in Saul's life, these two references make clear that his most dominant problem emotion was anger and resentment. It is a good rule in life that whenever you come across a dominant problem emotion of anger or resentment you say to yourself, *a goal here is being undermined and blocked.* If the dominant problem emotion is anxiety and fear–no doubt Saul's fear of his standing with his people–the goal is an uncertain one. It is probably reachable, but the person is not sure he or she can reach it, thus producing the emotion of anxiety. Saul feared for his tenure as king and for his heir Jonathan to take the throne.

Saul tried to shame Jonathan by insulting his mother and predicting that his kingdom would never be built. If Saul had succeeded in the dominant problem emotion of producing guilt and shame, then most likely Jonathan would have taken up his father's cause and pursued David as well. Instead, Jonathan remained true to David.

If you can think through problem emotions, you are catching on! We cannot be sure at this stage what Saul's goal was, but we know from the dominant emotions that it is likely to be a goal that he feels is being undermined and blocked. If so, what would you expect to happen? Next week we'll examine the ongoing consequences of Saul's emotions.

---

[1] Larry Crabb, as quoted in Selwyn Hughes, *Christ Empowered Living* (Nashville: Broadman & Holman, 2001), 118.

[2] Alfred Adler, as cited in Hughes, *Christ Empowered Living*, 116.

[3] Tennyson, as quoted in Hughes, *Christ Empowered Living*, 69.

[4] Kevin Hughes, *Parenting Adolescents* (Colorado Springs: Navpress, 1989), 190.

Session 5: *Restoring the Image*

1. A key issue to remember throughout this seminar is that God has put

   _____ in our hearts. As a result of this, everyone arrives in this world

   with _____ to get back to the way things were prior to the fall.

2. Remember, too, the simple formula that all behavior moves towards a _____,

   and whenever that _____ is undermined, uncertain, or unreachable, problem

   _____ arise in the personality.

3. No one can return to the original _____ by their own volition. There

   can be no _____ within the realm of _____.

4. Jesus Christ alone is the perfect _____-_____. He alone can

   truly and fully _____ God.

   Important Scriptures concerning the word *image:* 1 Corinthians 11:7-10;
   2 Corinthians 4:4-6; Colossians 1:15-16; Colossians 3:9-10; Hebrews 1:3

5. God wants to _____ us to the image of Jesus Christ.

6. Justification takes a moment, but sanctification is a _____ which

   takes time to work out.

7. Reconstruction cannot be achieved through self-effort. What we're talking

   about is not self-motivated living or self-engendered living. What we're talking

   about is _____-_____ _____.

8. We surveyed the five areas of functioning in relation to the _____ sin has

   done to our personalities, so now we must follow the same route to see how the

   damage can be corrected. The power needed for this comes only through

   _____ _____.

9. Consider first the relational aspect of our being.

    a. We are built for relationships and apart from them we have no way of

        realizing our _____. Relationship is the _____ of reality.

"The Father loves the Son and gives Him everything. The Son always does that which pleases the Father. The Spirit takes of the things of the Son and shows them to us. He does not glorify Himself. We learn from the Trinity that relationship is of the essence of reality and therefore of the essence of our own existence, and we also learn that the way this relationship should be expressed is by concern for others. ... Within the Trinity itself there is a concern by the Persons of the Trinity one for another"[1] (D. Broughton Knox).

    b. Only in relationship with God can the deepest _____ of our hearts be met.

    c. The way we relate to _____ will determine the way we relate to

        _____.

Scripture puts this point forcibly when it says: "If anyone says, 'I love God,' yet hates his brother, he is a liar. For anyone who does not love his brother, whom he has seen, cannot love God, whom he has not seen. And he has given us this command: Whoever loves God must also love his brother" (1 John 4:20-21).

        (1) Realize there is so much more to _____ about God but that we

            know so _____ about Him.

        (2) Seek to Him for who He _____, not just for what He _____.

    d. We must never forget that the richer our relationship with God, the richer it will be with others.

RESTORING THE IMAGE

✥

"Your attitude should be the same as that of Christ Jesus: Who, being in very nature God, did not consider equality with God something to be grasped, but made himself nothing, taking the very nature of a servant, being made in human likeness."

PHILIPPIANS 2:4-7

Imagine a great concert pianist attempting to play the Warsaw Concerto on a toy piano. The musical genius would be present, but the expression would be limited by the instrument. But now think of the same musician sitting before a modern grand piano. At once all his powers come into play, and as he weaves the melodies, you say to yourself, "Ah, what a great musician. The grand piano reveals him."

In much the same way the cross reveals the heart of God. Had Jesus simply lived on this earth without giving His life on a cross, history would have recorded that One came among us who lived as God designed life to be lived. Great though that would have been, there would have been no power in it to restore us to the image of God.

The Incarnation revealed God, but it took a cross to reconcile us to Him.

For nearly two thousand years Jesus Christ has been coming into the lives of men and women and transforming them. Some of the first to receive Him were adulterers, thieves, swindlers, and drunkards. Everyone needs the change Christ offers, for He is the supreme specialist in making men and women whole.

Christ-empowered living is not observing and imitating Jesus' earthly life; it is living that life through the power of Christ in you. How does that happen? What was God's plan for restoring fallen men and women?

As you read, look for answers to these key questions:
1. Why was Jesus the perfect Image-Bearer?
2. How did He reflect God's image relationally, rationally, volitionally, emotionally, and physically?
3. What is the process of restoration?

As we begin week 5 and set the stage for a major shift in our study, let's remind ourselves of what we have uncovered before we move on. The first man and woman were made in the image of God—a relational, rational, volitional, and emotional being; He made Adam and Eve with those same characteristics. The once-obedient will became rebellious. Instead of clearly reflecting God, Adam and Eve were as broken lenses reflecting broken light.

God made us to function best when we are in a relationship with Him. Adam and Eve broke that relationship and became disconnected from God. Because God has put eternity in our hearts, each of us arrives in this world with a longing to get back to the way things were before the fall. Every one of us longs for the security, self-worth, and significance for which we were made, and this longing is so powerful that if it is not met in our relationship with God, then we easily become vulnerable to other sources of satisfaction.

Because our minds are filled with foolishness, we think we know where life can be found, and we often walk past the Fountain of living Water to go out into a desert and try to slake our thirst in wells of our own making. It feels good to us to know that the water we drink is under our control.

Recall the definition of sin from week 2.

Sin is declaring _____ from God.

To drink of the life-giving water which is to be found only in God requires a degree of helplessness which our carnal nature abhors. We think we can experience life by acting independently of God. So with our foolish minds we think of wrong strategies for holding our lives together.

We are choosing beings also. With our unmet longings relentlessly driving us forward and our sinful beliefs guiding our search, we seek relief. The stage is set for a visible direction to emerge as we look for a way to handle our world and experience some degree of intactness in our souls. So we set goals which we pursue with passion. Remember the formula: whatever I believe will meet my need will become my goal.

Review the meaning of the word *goal* as it is used in this study.

A goal is an objective we pursue which we foolishly believe will enable us to experience the security, self-worth, and significance for which our souls so desperately long.

Write at least one goal that you set and accomplished yet did not find to be as satisfying as you had expected.

_____

_____

Whenever the goal we set for ourselves is undermined, unreachable, or uncertain, we experience emotions such as anger and resentment, guilt and shame, and fear and anxiety. Sometimes these emotions become so turbulent that they incapacitate us, causing us to seek help from others.

If ever this ruined instrument of our personalities is to be put together again, it can never be done from within ourselves. The record of the human race shows that none of us can bring ourselves back to the original design. Fallen humanity, in this dire situation and desolate ruin, needed a Deliverer.

THE DELIVERER

We come now to the turning point of our study. We have surveyed the damage that has been caused to our personalities by the fall. Now we are going to focus on how it can be overcome.

Throughout the Old Testament—in fact, ever since God promised that the seed of the woman would crush the serpent's head in Genesis 3:15—God kept alive the fact that one day a Deliverer would come. It is as though a trumpeter took his stand on the first of the turrets that form the 39 books of the Old Testament and announced the coming of the Savior: Get Ready, He is coming.

The ancient seers of God strained their eyes through the darkness of the future and caught the gleam of a coming light. They knew something wonderful was impending in heaven. Isaiah spoke for all the prophets, when looking forward and predicting the coming of the Messiah, he cried: "The people walking in darkness have seen a great light" (Isa. 9:2).

The Perfect Image-Bearer

"The Word became flesh and made his dwelling among us. We have seen his glory, the glory of the One and Only, who came from the Father, full of grace and truth."

—JOHN 1:14

Around 2,000 years ago that "great light" was seen on earth when God dwelt among us in the form of His Son. When Jesus came to earth as a baby and then grew in stature, He displayed in His personality the perfect representation of God. He was a perfect image-bearer. We said earlier that whatever that elusive word *personality* might mean, the least it could mean is that a person can relate, think, choose, and feel.

Nowhere did the image of God shine more clearly and more perfectly in human form than in the life and person of Jesus of Nazareth. In Jesus the great Triune God comes nearest to our understanding.

The expression "the image of God" never occurs in the Old Testament after the account of creation except in Genesis 9. In the New Testament, however, it appears several times.

Read the following Scriptures. Explain how each supports the idea that Jesus bore the image of God.

2 Corinthians 4:4 _____

Colossians 1:15 _____

Hebrews 1:3 _____

How perfectly did Christ display the image of God on earth? You have
only to look through the pages of the Gospels to see that He was totally
dependent on God for everything. He stayed close to God in prayer, He
studied the Scriptures, thought clearly about everything, always made the
right decisions, and exhibited a perfect emotional balance. The personality
of Jesus was, in fact, the kind of personality that God had in mind for
every one of His creations—a personality that functioned according to the
divine design. Relationally, rationally, volitionally, emotionally and physically, Jesus was the best reflector of God's image the world has ever seen.

> The personality of Jesus was, in fact, the kind of personality that God had in mind for every one of His creations.

Perfect Relationally

Perhaps nowhere is our Lord's perfection seen more clearly than in the
way He related to people. In the Gospels, we see Jesus often surrounded
by crowds. Children flocked to Him, and He gathered them in His arms.
In all the contacts Jesus made with women, He was always respectful.

> **Jesus' ministry grew out of relationships. Which of the following was
> Jesus' priority in beginning His public ministry? To check your answer
> read Matthew 4:18-20, Mark 1:16-18, or John 1:35-37.**
> ❑ Established headquarters in Capernaum
> ❑ Healed many to attract followers
> ❑ Called the twelve disciples
> ❑ Solicited funds from key leaders

Look how He related to His disciples. They were all ordinary men. Yet He
took these men, and through His relationship with them, made them into a
powerful force in establishing His church.

A Unique Following
Repeatedly we read statements like this: "The people thronged around Him."
"They could not get near to Him because of the crowd." "The multitude
followed Him." Early in Jesus' ministry, except on those occasions when
He withdrew to pray, He seemed always to be in the midst of a crowd.

Children quickly sense the nature of an individual and are drawn to
those who are warm and friendly. Children flocked to Jesus, and He gathered them in His arms.

The Gospels are rich in incidents of Jesus relating to women—and
never did He imply their inferiority. Our Lord was born among a people
who took a low view of women. A Jew would not greet a woman on the
street—much less talk with her there. In morning prayer a male Jew
thanked God that he was not made a Gentile, a slave, or a woman. It was
impious for a Jewish man to teach a woman. Yet in all the contacts Jesus
made with women, He was always respectful.

A Unique Approach

The way in which our Lord built strong relationships with His disciples can be seen most clearly in an incident recorded for us in John 6. Christ had presented a challenging message to the crowd who had gathered to listen to Him. He talked about the fact that those who followed Him must be prepared to "eat his flesh and drink his blood."

The figure of speech He used was not understood by the people, and obviously they were offended by it. "From this time many of his disciples turned back and no longer followed him" (v. 66). The passage in John 6 continues: " 'You do not want to leave too, do you?' Jesus asked the Twelve. Simon Peter answered him, 'Lord, to whom shall we go? You have the words of eternal life. We believe and know that you are the Holy One of God' " (vv. 67-69).

It was a critical moment in the Master's career. The crowds who had flocked to hear Him were melting away, upset by His hard sayings. Reading the unspoken thoughts of His immediate band of disciples, Jesus brought the issue out into the open by asking, " 'You do not want to leave too, do you?' " (v. 67).

Seen against such a background, Peter's answer is magnificent. Peter realized that there was no one quite like Jesus. Peter had walked with Jesus and seen Him in all kinds of situations and circumstances, and never once had the Savior revealed any character flaws or committed any sin. Here was someone who related to God and others, not just effectively but perfectly. Is it any wonder that Peter responded the way he did? "Lord, to whom shall we go? You have the words of eternal life."

Perfect Rationally

At about 30 years of age, Jesus left Nazareth to become an itinerant preacher, but after a few months, He returned and visited the synagogue on the Sabbath day. He spoke to the congregation, and as they listened to Him, they were astonished at His words. Someone asked, " 'What's this wisdom that has been given him. … Isn't this the carpenter?' " (Mark 6:2-3). And when He spoke in the temple courts in Jerusalem, the Jews were amazed and said about Him, " 'How did this man get such learning without having studied?' " (John 7:15).

Notice how Jesus answered that question: " 'My teaching is not my own. It comes from him who sent me' " (v. 16). He continued, " 'If anyone chooses to do God's will, he will find out whether my teaching comes from God or whether I speak on my own' " (v. 17). The one who does the will of God perfectly is the one who understands all mysteries. The psalmist put it this way:

> *The LORD confides in those who fear him;*
> *he makes his covenant known to them (Ps. 25:14).*

Jesus alone perfectly does the will of God and is the one who understands all mysteries. He is familiar with things that those who disobey God's will can never comprehend.

Perfect Emotionally

Our Lord was perfect also in His emotional nature. His mind, seeing God perfectly, loved Him supremely. An unclouded intelligence will always result in a perfect consciousness of God. As our Lord Himself put it: " 'Blessed are the pure in heart, for they will see God' " (Matt. 5:8).

Because there was no impurity in Jesus, He saw God clearly. Carefully note and understand this sequence: What our minds engage greatly affects the way we feel, and how we feel greatly influences the way we act. Our Lord's unclouded intelligence brought about a perfect consciousness of God that captured His whole heart, soul, and mind. The One who saw God clearly loved Him perfectly. Jesus entertained no undivided affection.

Many other windows in the Gospels illuminates our Lord's emotional nature. Recall His whole being shaken with the emotion of grief and sadness as He beheld Jerusalem, the city He loved, hastening to its doom (Luke 19:41). Those tears were not just the perfect expression of Christ; they were also the perfect expression of God. The Savior felt as God felt.

Perfect Volitionally

Read Philippians 2:4-7 in the margin. More is revealed in this passage than just Christ's attitude of mind; we see also the act of will by which His change from heaven to earth was wrought. In the face of tremendous need, Jesus did not hold on to His right of equality; but for the purposes of your salvation and mine, He abandoned the privileges of the eternal throne to take upon Himself human flesh.

What did Jesus give up? What did He get in return?

Gave up   **Got**

_____   _____

_____   _____

"Each of you should look not only to your own interests, but also to the interests of others.
Your attitude should be the same as that of Christ Jesus:
Who, being in very nature God,
did not consider equality with God something to be grasped,
but made himself nothing, taking the very nature of a servant,
being made in human likeness."
—PHILIPPIANS 2:4-7

The action of Jesus' will is seen in those strange but sublime words "but made himself nothing." The eternal Word came from the bosom of the Father to the body of a woman, from a position where He had infinite expression to a state where He was limited in so many ways. The Word passed from controlling the universe to obedience, from independent cooperation in the equality of Deity to dependent submission to the will of God.

Jesus' will always chose the principle of divine activity, always moved toward the goal of pleasing God. In Romans 15:3, Paul told us Christ did not please Himself. Our Lord himself said on one occasion, " 'I seek not to please myself but him who sent me' " (John 5:30).

Jesus also said, " 'My food, ... is to do the will of him who sent me and to finish his work' " (John 4:34). Every movement and decision of the will of Jesus, under the constraint of the divine will, are a revelation of the action and method of the will of God, under the constraint of eternal love.

In Jesus we have a picture of a will yielded to the divine will in a way that is absolutely stupendous. In everything Jesus Christ did, He sought always to please the Father.

Becoming like Christ

Romans 8:29 is a wonderful verse: "Those God foreknew he also predestined to be conformed to the likeness of his Son, that he might be the firstborn among many brothers."

God wants to conform us to the image of Jesus Christ. God is so excited about Jesus that He wants to make everyone like Him. Just as the first Adam produced a son in his own likeness and after his own image (Gen 5:3) so the Last Adam—by His entrance into this world, His death on the cross, His resurrection from the dead, His ascension into heaven, and His sending back the Holy Spirit—is producing a progeny that bears a spiritual resemblance to Himself. The fall marred God's image in man, and Jesus' purpose is to restore it.

If you wanted to be the greatest in these areas, whom would you choose as a model?

TV star _____   Business tycoon _____

Sports star _____   Singer/Musician _____

Jesus is God's perfect man. Every facet of His wisdom reveals the wisdom of God. Every manifestation of His love is the revelation of a mind given over to God, a heart that is fully in love with God and a will working under the constraint of eternal love. Through Jesus God takes hold of mankind; through Jesus mankind takes hold of God.

The Process of Restoration

The reconstruction of our personalities begins when we come to the cross. Because it was at the cross that Christ paid the penalty for our sin, it is only there that God will meet with us. Once we come to the cross and receive forgiveness for our sins, the Bible says we are *justified*.

What does it mean to be justified? Well, to beautify means to be made beautiful; to pacify is to make peaceful; to justify is to be made just. It means more than being forgiven; it means we are credited with Christ's life and power. That's the first act in restoring us to the image of God—being justified.

But another word is used in the New Testament—a word that describes something more than an act, but a process. That word is *sanctification*. It takes a moment for justification to take place, but it takes a process for our personalities to be shaped in the image of Christ.

The first act in restoring us to the image of God is being justified.

Now let us be clear about this: reconstruction of the personality is not something we can achieve on our own. It can only be achieved as we draw close to Christ and avail ourselves of the power of the Holy Spirit. It is Christ-empowered living we are talking about, not self-empowered living.

So how does the process of the reconstruction of our personalities take place? What do we need to understand and do to function according to the divine design? Well, just as we went through the five functions of the personality to see how deeply the damage has been done to us by the fall, we must now follow the same route in looking at how that damage can be corrected through the power which comes to us through Jesus Christ.

The Relational Restoration

First we must look at the relational aspect of our beings. Fix it clearly in your mind that God has built you for relationships; He has designed us to first relate to Him, and then with others. The first movement of the soul toward completeness must always be in God's direction. The better we relate to God, the better we will relate to others.

The better we relate to God, the better we will relate to others.

If we do not relate well to God, then we are apt to move into relationships to *get* rather than to *give,* and we manipulate others to get what we ought really to be drawing from God. Three facts need to be expressed.

1. Relationship is the essence of reality.
We are built for relationships, and apart from them we have no way of realizing our potential. One theologian said that relationships are the essence of reality. The concept that God is a relational being and that there is perfect society in the godhead was brought home most forcibly to me many years ago in a paragraph I read in a small book entitled *The Everlasting God.* "The Father loves the Son and gives Him everything. The Son always does that which pleases the Father. The Spirit takes of the things of the Son and shows them to us. He does not glorify Himself. We learn from the Trinity that relationship is of the essence of reality and therefore of the essence of our own existence, and we also learn that the way this relationship should be expressed is by concern for others. … Within the Trinity itself there is a concern by the Persons of the Trinity one for another."[2]

That insight brought one of the greatest paradigm shifts in my thinking that I have ever experienced. I had always believed that truth was the essence of reality, but here was a reputable theologian saying that the basic nature of reality is not truth, but relationships. The more I considered it, the more right it seemed. This insight changed my whole approach to God, to people, and to the Bible.

Does this mean that truth is unimportant? No, because it is truth that brings us to reality. C. S. Lewis put it like this: "Truth is always about something, but reality is that about which truth is."[3] Reality, when we find it, has to do with perfect relationships. Truth cannot be fully grasped in sentences, it can be fully comprehended only in relationships.

I like what Dr. Larry Crabb says about this point: "If one believes that God exists as three persons who are distinct enough to actually relate to one another then it becomes clear somehow that the final nature of things is wrapped up in the idea of relationship. The essence of what it means to exist, the center of everything, the core of ontology, can no longer be thought of in individual terms. ... There is relationship within the very nature of God. God is a personal being who exists eternally in a relationship among persons. He is His own community."[4]

Read Matthew 3:16-17 in the margin. All three are present—Jesus, the dove representing the Holy Spirit, and the Father's voice. What seem to be the dominant attitudes of the Trinity's relationship? (underline)
Joy   Love   Appreciation   Encouragement   Admiration

Ultimate reality, therefore, is personal and not propositional. In heaven we will not be discussing truth or doctrine but relating in the way the Trinity relates: beautifully, perfectly, eternally. No arguments, no quarrels, no dissension. Whatever else the three persons of the Trinity do, nothing can be more important than the fact that they maintain within and among themselves perfect other-centered relationships.

2. Our deepest longings are met only in relationship with God.
We simply have to get hold of this fact. Nothing, or no one but Jesus Christ can satisfy these longings in such a way that the soul feels fully satisfied. Material things, our loved ones, and our best friends cannot satisfy these longings. The finest relationships we can experience here on earth are incapable of meeting our souls' deepest needs. Because God has set eternity in our hearts, every one of us reaches out to Him—even the most hardened atheist. Such a person would not admit it, of course. An atheist said to me, "I don't believe in God, but I would like to if only to satisfy the desire in me for transcendence."

How do we look to God to experience the security, self-worth, and significance our souls need to function effectively? Consider the first essential, security—which we said means a sense of being loved. Often a person has said to me, "my problem is that I don't love the Lord enough." My usual reply is, "No, that is not your problem. Your problem is that you don't know how much the Lord loves you."

If you don't feel you love God enough, what might be the condition of your heart? Check one or more.
❑ Anger toward God   ❑ Comfort zone at present
❑ Unconfessed sin   ❑ Poor self-esteem
❑ Disappointment with God   ❑ Misplaced priorities

Love for God and His Son Jesus Christ is not something we manufacture in our souls but something that is a response. Scripture says in 1 John 4:19, "We love because he first loved us." Christians who think they have to cultivate a love for God in their hearts are going about it the wrong way. As we allow our hearts to focus on the cross and what God has done for

"As soon as Jesus was baptized, he went up out of the water. At that moment heaven was opened, and he saw the Spirit of God descending like a dove and lighting on him. And a voice from heaven said, 'This is my Son, whom I love; with him I am well pleased.' "
—MATTHEW 3:16-17

us there, the Holy Spirit delights to give us a blinding revelation of God's love. Seeing how much we are loved, the scales fall from our eyes, and our own love flames in response.

Heaven knows no higher strategy for begetting love in mortal hearts than by bringing us to the cross, revealing to us what it cost God to save us. The vision of that love flows into our hearts, bringing us a deep sense of security. Nothing holds us fast and secure in the swirling currents of life like knowing we are loved. When we feel loved, we can rise above our grudges and give up our resentment.

3. The way we relate to God determines how we relate to others.
How do we develop our relationship with God? In the same way that we develop our relationship with our fellow human beings—we spend time with them. Permit me to ask you: how much time do you spend in getting to know God? How much time do you spend in prayer or in reading His word? These are the two priorities in knowing God—spending time in prayer and reading His Word. Fail there and we fail all along the line.

The psalmist said in Psalm 42:1-2:

> *As the deer pants for streams of water,*
> *so my soul pants for you, O God.*
> *My soul thirsts for God, for the living God.*
> *When can I go and meet with God?*

How did the psalmist come to say that his soul panted after God? The image is powerful and strong. He says something similar in other Psalms:

> *O God, you are my God,*
> *earnestly I seek you;*
> *my soul thirsts for you,*
> *my body longs for you,*
> *in a dry and weary land*
> *where there is no water (Ps. 63:1).*

> *I spread out my hands to you;*
> *my soul thirsts for you like a parched land. (Ps. 143:6).*

Could you say in all honesty that your soul pants after God? Most of us would say we love God, we desire to know Him better—but pant after Him? What does it mean to pant after God? I think it means three things:

1. Getting to know God
Panting after God means realizing that there is much about God to know but that we know so little. The Apostle Paul, a man who knew more about God than most, cried out in his epistle to the Philippians: "I want to know Christ and the power of his resurrection and the fellowship of sharing in his sufferings, becoming like him in his death" (3:10).

Someone has said that the beginning of education is the realization of one's ignorance. It is the same in one's spiritual life. The beginning of spiritual development is the realization of how little of God we know and a willingness and a desire to pursue Him.

2. Making God our central focus

When we make God our soul's central focus, we will pant after Him. This means much more than attending church on Sunday, making sure we say our prayers before going to sleep, or occasionally reading a passage from Scripture. It means lingering before Him, feeding our soul as much as we can on His Word, and meditating in that Word.

3. Seeking to know Him for who He is

Panting after God means seeking to know Him for who He is, not just for what He gives. We are often more interested in the hands of God than the face of God. We focus more on asking Him for things than just gazing on Him with delight.

"I want to know Christ and the power of his resurrection and the fellowship of sharing in his sufferings, becoming like him in his death, and so, somehow, to attain to the resurrection from the dead."

—Philippians 3:10

> **Place an X on the line to indicate which aspect of God you most often seek in prayer and worship.**
>
> |————————————————————————————————|
>
> Hands of God   Face of God
> (Getting)   (Knowing)

So ask yourself: How deeply do you desire to know God? To what lengths are you prepared to go to know Him better?

The soul is capable of great passion; we see this in great music and art. We are designed to be drawn to God, to pant after God. In my opinion, nothing is sadder than to see a Christian taken up only with the duties of the Christian life and lacking a passionate, even romantic relationship with God and His Son Jesus Christ. Let's never forget that the richer our relationship with God, the richer it will be with others.

The richer our relationship with God, the richer it will be with others.

Learning from the Mistakes of Others

Last week we unearthed the negative emotional state of King Saul's heart. We said that Saul was chasing a goal that might prove to be undermined and blocked. Did he have a history of making right choices? Let's see.

Volitional Evidences

First Samuel 15 records one of the clearest possible pictures of King Saul's volitional capacity at work. It begins with the prophet Samuel instructing Saul to destroy the Amalekites because of their enmity toward Israel. The instructions were crystal clear: " 'Now go, attack the Amalekites and totally destroy everything that belongs to them. Do not spare them; put to death men and women, children and infants, cattle and sheep, camels and donkeys' " (1 Sam. 15:3).

Saul, however, decided to willfully disobey God by sparing the leader of the Amalekites—King Agag—and also the best of the sheep. "Saul and the army spared Agag and the best of the sheep and cattle, the fat calves and lambs—everything that was good. These they were unwilling to destroy completely, but everything that was despised and weak they totally destroyed" (1 Sam. 15:9).

Samuel confronted King Saul over his disobedience whereupon Saul rationalized the situation by saying that the best of the sheep were spared in order to sacrifice them to the Lord at Gilgal (v. 21). A rationalization is usually a plausible but irrelevant reason for one's actions.

Samuel's response was to remind Saul that when God gives instructions, He wants them obeyed. Not to obey them is willful disobedience.

Then came the solemn words:

> *"To obey is better than sacrifice,*
> *and to heed is better than the fat of rams.*
> *For rebellion is like the sin of divination,*
> *and arrogance like the evil of idolatry" (1 Sam. 15:22-23).*

By excluding Agag and allowing the people to keep the best of the cattle from destruction, the clear intent of the commands was violated. God's plans were amended to leave room for the least little bit of royal vanity. God commanded the war to remove the threat of a godless and hostile way of life, but Saul conducted it in terms of his own ideas. Agag was a prize among the spoils. A live Agag looked better than a dead one.

The oracle to obey is picked up many times in Scripture—more than a hundred times. Following Samuel's confrontation, Saul appears to repent. Listen to what he says: "Then Saul said to Samuel, 'I have sinned. I violated the Lord's command and your instructions. I was afraid of the people and so I gave in to them. Now I beg you, forgive my sin and come back with me, so that I may worship the Lord' " (v. 24-25).

It looked like repentance, but Samuel saw that Saul was *remorseful* rather than *repentant*. He was sorry for what had happened but not sorry for the underlying cause of his sin.

Since all behavior moves toward a goal, what might King Saul's goal have been in behaving the way he did in this chapter? We'll discuss the answer in next week's study.

---

[1] D. Broughton Knox, *The Everlasting God* (Welwyn, England:Evangelical Press, 1982), 64.
[2] Ibid.
[3] C. S. Lewis, as quoted in Selwyn Hughes, *Christ Empowered Living* (Nashville: Broadman & Holman, 2001), 10.
[4] Larry Crabb, as quoted in Hughes, *Christ Empowered Living*, 11.

Session 6: The Dynamic of Change

❧

In this session we come to grips with the way change takes place in the personality.

1. The three main theories about change:

    a. Getting _____ about ourselves.

    b. When our efforts bring no _____.

    c. Moving _____ to God.

2. There are several issues that need to be understood in relation to this issue of deep spiritual change:

    a. A clear understanding and awareness of _____.

    b. A willingness to own up to the _____ of sin.

    c. A turning away from sin through real and radical _____.

First, a clear understanding and awareness of sin

1. We cannot comprehend the nature of sin until we see it as _____-

_____—the ego in the place God has reserved for Himself.

2. Every human heart has been invaded by _____. It seeks to turn God

out of the very universe He created.

3. Sin is not just conscious _____ towards God; it is also the

relegation of God to _____.

Second, a willingness to own up to the reality of sin in our lives

1. The biblical term for this concept is _____.

2. General confessions which are vague and unspecific are not worth much.

In times of revival people begin to confess _____ sins.

3. We may pass many tests on the outside, but can we pass the test of

_____ _____?

Third, moving closer to God

1. A concept we need to understand in relation to moving closer to God is that

of _____.

2. What repentance is not:

    a. Repentance is not _____   c. Repentance is not _____

    b. Repentance is not _____   d. Repentance is not _____

3. What is repentance? Repentance comes from the Greek word *metanoia,* which

means a _____ of _____.

Consider Hosea 14:1-3 which unfolds for us what is required in repentance.

4. Three things ought to be in our minds as we consider the act of repentance.

    a. Our failure to trust God's _____.

    b. Our failure to believe God's evaluation of our _____.

    c. Our failure to see underlying _____ or _____ in our lives.

5. Never be satisfied with _____ repentance—lopping off the

_____ rather than demolishing the _____.

6. Repentance ought not be an _____ thing in our lives. It ought

to be a regular occurrence.

7. Repentance, when properly understood, is a _____.

Week Six

THE DYNAMIC OF CHANGE

❖

"If we claim to be without sin, we deceive ourselves and the truth is not in us. If we confess our sins, he is faithful and just and will forgive us our sins and purify us from all unrighteousness."

I JOHN 1:8-9

Earlier we talked about sin in general terms. Now we must give it a sharper focus. It's no coincidence that the two main words in the Bible for sin are the Hebrew *chata* and the Greek *harmartia*. Both mean *missing the mark*.

Gerald Kennedy, in a book called *The Parables,* tells of an old man in Arkansas who was a compulsive sharpshooter. He would take pot shots at anything in sight. A skilled marksman following his trail was surprised always to find a bull's-eye. Wherever he went, he found signs of the sharpshooter's exploits—a barn door, a ranch fencing, or wherever—there was always a circle traced in white chalk and right in the center a bullet hole.

This impressed the observer immensely. Meeting up with the old man, he complimented him on his superb marksmanship. The sharpshooter made light of it, and with a wave of his hand he dismissed it. "Shucks," he said, "'tain't nothing. I jess shoots first and draws a circle afterwards!"[1]

Like the sharpshooter, many people try to define sin on their own terms and then draw a circle around it to shut out God's truth. Christians who want to experience Christ-empowered living must open themselves to God's scrutiny and practice a lifestyle of confession and repentance.

As you read, keep these questions in mind:
1. What is a clear definition of sin?
2. Why should we be willing to admit the reality of sin in our lives?
3. What is the difference between remorse and repentance?

How does change take place in the personality? All kinds of theories are to be found on this subject. Some say we are changed when we get some insight about ourselves. Others say we change when we see that what we do does not bring us any rewards. The greatest trigger for change in a Christian's heart is when he determines to move closer to God. The greatest change comes about in the human personality in a restored relationship with God.

Three issues need to be understood in order to experience this change:
1. A clear understanding and awareness of sin
2. A willingness to own up to the reality of sin in one's life
3. A turning away from sin through real and radical repentance

The greatest trigger for change is to move closer to God.

Clear Understanding and Awareness of Sin

One of the alarming trends in today's society is the death of the concept of sin. Cornelius Plantinga, Jr. in his book *The Breviary of Sin* says: "The awareness of sin used to be our shadow. Christians hated sin, feared it, fled from it, grieved over it. ... But the shadow has dimmed. Nowadays, the accusation 'you have sinned' is often said with a grin, and with a tone that signals an inside joke. At one time, this accusation still had the power to jolt people. Catholics lined up to confess their sins; Protestant preachers rose up to confess *our* sins. And they did it regularly. As a child growing up in the fifties ... I think I heard as many sermons about sin as I did about grace. The assumption in those days seemed to be that you couldn't understand either without understanding both."[2]

Modern-day living has shaped the human, and even to some degree the Christian, concept of sin. Our "self-deception about our sin acts is a narcotic, a tranquilizing and disorienting suppression of our spiritual central nervous system."[3] Because of the lack of awareness of sin in the human race, a Savior is seen as quaint in today's world.

When we lack an ear for the wrong notes we cannot play the right ones or recognize them in the performance of others. We become so nonmusical that we miss the exposition and recapitulation of the main themes which God plays in human life. The music of creation leaves us with no catch of our breath. Mere beauty begins to bore us.

So what is sin? The Bible presents the concept of sin in an array of different images: missing a target, wandering from the path, straying from the fold, blindness, deafness, and overstepping a line of railing to reach the goal that God has set for our lives. Personally, I do not think we can comprehend the nature of sin until we see it as self-centerdness—the ego occupying the place that God has reserved for Himself.

To understand what sin is all about we need to chop off the first and last letters of the word. And what are we left with? I—which has been called the perpendicular pronoun. See the letter in your imagination, and raise it to cosmic proportions in your mind. See it standing tall and stiff and starched. That is what sin is—the ego standing proud and defiant in the face of the universe saying, "I don't want anyone else telling me what to do. I want to live my life the way I want."

Explain how these sins represent the self-centered ego in charge.

Cheating on taxes _____

Padding expense reports _____

Inventing an excuse for being late _____

Taking credit for someone else's work _____

If I were to look at the human personality from a three-dimensional point of view, it would consist of body, soul, and spirit. Sin is self at the center rather than God. Many Christians see sin in terms of adultery, fornication, lying, stealing, cheating, and so on; but sin is subtle as well as obvious. Sin is pushing God out of the center, the controlling part our of our lives which He designed to be inhabited by Himself.

You and I have been invaded by a principle called pride, which wants to maintain our independence and refuses to yield control to another—the other being God. That principle of pride, if pushed to its nth degree, reveals the depravity that is in our hearts and spotlights what pride did to the Son of God. The cross sought to turn Him out of the very universe He created.

Sin is not just conscious hostility to God; it is also the relegation of God to irrelevance. I doubt whether there is anyone reading this now (it may be so of course) who is consciously hostile to God, but how many of us relegate Him to the margin of our lives, live independently of Him until a crisis develops, and then attempt to put Him back in the center.

If you had a day (24 hours) you could enjoy with anyone of your choosing, who would it be? Rank your choices by listing the number of hours with each.

Friend ____ hrs.   Celebrity ____ hrs.

Spouse ____ hrs.   Other family member____ hrs.

God ____ hrs.   Self ____ hrs.

How sad that, although we are Christians, we can allow our thinking to drift toward the notion that our security, self-worth, and significance depend on our performance or accomplishments. We tend to search for a deeper level of confidence than God, something we can see, something we can touch, something other than the invisible God.

We pay lip service to the fact that Christ is the source of satisfaction yet we continue to drink of lukewarm, bacteria-infected wells of our own making because we like to live independently of God and be in control of the water that we drink. Such actions relegate God to irrelevance.

The cross sought to turn Him out of the very universe He created.

Willingness to Own Up to Sin

Let me pick up on the second concept—a willingness to own up to the reality of sin in our lives. The term we use for this is *confession*. King David in the Old Testament put it like this:

> *Then I acknowledged my sin to you*
> *and did not cover up my iniquity.*
> *I said, "I will confess*
> *my transgressions to the LORD"—*
> *and you forgave*
> *the guilt of my sin (Ps. 32:5).*

General confessions that are vague and unspecific are not worth very much. One of the characteristics of classic revival—a subject I have studied for most of my life—is that in revival people begin to confess specific sins.

During the revival on Hebrides, one of the isles of Scotland, in the middle of the last century a young man stood up in a prayer meeting and said: "Lord it is so much humbug when we say we have sinned, our hands are unclean. *I* have sinned, *my* hands are unclean. Forgive me. Oh forgive me." At this point he broke down in tears and soon others followed, confessing specific sins that were going on in their lives.

An old English proverb says, "Confession is good for the soul." An old Puritan preacher said, "We must own our sin in order that we may disown it." When we are ready to uncover our sin, then God is ready to cover it. The writer of the book of Proverbs put it like this:

> *He who conceals his sins does not prosper,*
> *but whoever confesses and renounces them finds mercy*
> *(Prov. 28:13).*

I think the Apostle John puts it best when he says, "If we confess our sins, he is faithful and just and will forgive us our sins and purify us from all unrighteousness" (1 John 1:9).

It is likely that many reading this now, myself included, may not be conscious of any great sins in our lives. We may live what we consider to be good Christian lives, read our Bible regularly if not daily, spend time with God in prayer, give to God's work, involve ourselves in good works, refrain from bad habits, and so on. But how many of us can honestly say that we find our security, self-worth, and significance in Him?

Sin is subtle. We can pass all the tests on the outside but easily pass over misplaced dependency inside. As we said before, the root of sin is pushing God out of the part He made for Himself.

I do not believe our lives will come together in the way God desires until we admit that far too often we run out lives on our own terms. My security, self-worth, and significance are things I want to establish myself, rather than trusting God with them.

When we are ready to uncover our sin, then God is ready to cover it.

One of the biggest challenges of our lives is engaging God around the issues of security, self-worth, and significance. It is possible for other sins to be absent in our lives but for the root of it—misplaced dependency—to be lying there.

If you had said to me when I was a young pastor, "Do you trust God with your life?" I would have said, "Of course I do." Ask me now, and I would have to say, "some of the time." I struggle with the same problem that the ancient Israelites had—whether to look to God to satisfy the ache in their souls or whether to dig wells and find some other means of satisfying the thirst in the soul.

To what extent is misplaced dependency a problem for you? Place an X on the line for each aspect of your life.

	Trust myself Trust God
Providing for my family	⊢————————————⊣
Finding a better job	⊢————————————⊣
Managing my expenses	⊢————————————⊣
Managing my time	⊢————————————⊣
Choosing friends	⊢————————————⊣
Choosing entertainment	⊢————————————⊣

This principle of pride, present in every one of our hearts, if taken to its nth degree, seeks to dethrone God. If you have difficulty seeing it in those terms, then consider the cross. One of the purposes of the cross is to make us see plainly what is normally hidden, the foulness and deadly nature of the principle of pride.

What were those ordinary sins? There was the bigotry of the Pharisees. Who hasn't been bigoted? There was the self-seeking of the Sadducees. Who has not been self-seeking? There was the indifference of the crowd. And who has not been indifferent? Add up all the other ordinary sins that come to mind, and underlying them you will find pride—the desire to put self-interest before God's interests.

We would never have understood what pride could do until we saw it at the cross. It would never enter our minds that pride could lead to that situation. But it could, and it did.

Add up the ordinary sins and you will find pride—the desire to put self-interest before God's interests.

Turning Away from Sin Through Repentance

The next word we need to examine is the word *repentance*. I have been astonished in my years as a minister and counselor at how few Christians understand what repentance is all about. I did a survey on one occasion among a group of mature Christians to determine how they understood repentance. Some thought repentance was something we did at conversion —a one-time thing—and never needs to be done again. Others came up with descriptions of different states of mind that came close to repentance, but only a small minority understood the real meaning of the word.

What Repentance Is Not

In order to understand what something is, it's often helpful to begin with what it's not. Let me follow that model in relation to the word *repentance*.

1. Repentance is not regret.

Regret is being sorry for oneself, deploring the consequences of one's actions. In the United Kingdom we once had an archbishop by the name of William Temple. Before ordaining priests to the Christian ministry, he customarily asked them to define repentance. One young ordinand said "repentance is a heart broken by sin." "Nonsense," said the archbishop. "Repentance is a heart that has broken away from sin." It is one thing to regret what has happened; it is another thing to do something about it.

2. Repentance is not remorse.

Remorse has been described as sorrow without hope at its heart. The great early church father Tertullian said that remorse is an emotion of disgust. Judas was remorseful but refused to return to Christ and ask forgiveness. Remorse eats its heart out without seeking a new heart.

> Remorse eats its heart out without seeking a new heart.

3. Repentance is not reformation.

When they feel the need for change, some people try to achieve it by self-effort. They turn over a new leaf and attempt to become reformed characters. You may remember that in the church at Ephesus, which our Lord addresses in the Book of Revelation, He commands them to return to doing their first works. But before saying that, He commanded them to repent. Reformation may follow repentance in the sense that we attend to the things that need putting right in our lives, but it can never precede it.

4. Repentance is not reparation (making amends).

Anyone who truly repents, like Zacchaeus in the Gospels, will seek to make amends to those who were wronged, when possible and appropriate. Scripture talks about producing " 'fruit in keeping with repentance' " (Matt. 3:8). This issue is often overlooked by some spiritual advisors, but it is clearly a scriptural principle whenever possible to make amends for what we might have done wrong. This, however, is reparation not repentance. Once again reparation must follow repentance, not precede it.

Real Repentance

So what is repentance? The Greek word for *repentance* is *metanoia*, meaning *after knowledge* as distinguished from *pronoia* meaning *foreknowledge*. The word literally means *a change of mind.*

Repentance literally means *a change of mind.*

Label the following as *T* for true repentance and *F* for false repentance.

___ Lord, I am sorry for what I did wrong, but I was under a lot of pressure at the time.

___ Lord, life is difficult. I will try to do better next time.

___ Lord, I wish I didn't fall into sin so easily. It's tough out there.

___ Lord, give me grace not to fall into sin the way I have just done.

Many apologies sound sincere but really have a scapegoat built in. They allow the one asking for forgiveness to get off the hook. In the previous learning activity, all of the statements were false repentances. True repentance is a demonstrated change.

The Christian psychiatrist John White says, "repentance is a changed way of looking at things."[4] He defines *repentance* as the shock that comes from seeing reality. It is indeed a shock when you discover that although you are a Christian, you are living independently of the life offered to you in Christ and are attempting to find security, significance, and self-worth in things other than Christ.

The full realization of this, brought about through the intervention of the Holy Spirit, can be like an earthquake in the soul. When talking about repentance, C. S. Lewis said, "It's just as it was when you passed it before, but your eyes are altered. You see nothing now but realities."[5]

The Apostle Paul said in Romans 2:4, "Do you show contempt for the riches of his kindness, tolerance and patience, not realizing that God's kindness leads you toward repentance?" A realization of God's provision of physical and spiritual resources makes us aware that He alone can provide the security and significance we long for. When we become aware that we have ignored His sufficiency, we develop a godly sorrow that brings repentance (see 2 Cor. 7:10).

What is involved in an act of repentance? Let me take you to a wonderful passage in the Book of Hosea which I believe unfolds for us what is required in repentance.

> *Return, O Israel, to the LORD your God.*
>   *Your sins have been your downfall!*
>
> *Take words with you*
>   *and return to the LORD.*
> *Say to him:*
>   *"Forgive all our sins*
> *and receive us graciously,*
>   *that we may offer the fruit of our lips.*
> *Assyria cannot save us;*
>   *we will not mount war-horses.*
> *We will never again say 'Our gods'*
>   *to what our own hands have made" (Hos. 14:1-3).*

Let's examine it phrase by phrase. "Return ... to the LORD your God. Your sins have been your downfall" (v. 1). Sin is a movement away from God, and any return to God requires a 180-degree turn toward God. A 90-degree turn is not enough. Repentance, said C. S. Lewis in his book *Mere Christianity,* is a "movement full speed astern."[6] It is not just putting things right; it is coming back into a renewed relationship with God.

Draw a stick figure on the center of the line. Then draw a directional arrow that represents movement away from God (sin). Next draw a directional arrow that represents full repentance. Then draw a third directional arrow that represents partial repentance.

God ————————————————————————— Sin

Is it possible to partially repent? ❑ Yes ❑ No

"Your sins have been your downfall!" (v. 1). Hosea said you have stumbled because of your iniquity. Never tamper with the labels when it comes to sin. No euphemisms. It must be called by its proper name—iniquity. To spurn God's grace and rely instead on our own resources is not merely a spiritual infraction; it is iniquity. And it must be seen as such.

"Return to the Lord," says Hosea (v. 2). This Scripture emphasizes the fact once again that true repentance is returning to a relationship with God—a relationship that has been broken by sin such as the sin of misplaced dependency. Someone has said, "Maturity is where you place your dependency." Repentance enables us to mend our relationship with God through asking His forgiveness.

"Receive us graciously, that we may offer the fruit of our lips" (v. 2). The purpose of repentance is to restore us to a right relationship with God so that we can worship Him in spirit and in truth and draw daily on His grace. In Old Testament days an animal sacrifice was made to atone for sin, but what God longed for was a sacrifice of praise arising from a realized awareness of forgiveness. Where an attitude of thankfulness for sins forgiven is absent, true worship cannot exist.

"Assyria cannot save us" (v. 3). Assyria had become an international power during Hosea's time, but for the nation to look to them when they needed help rather than putting their trust in God was misplaced dependency.

"We will not mount war-horses" (v. 3). Israel was expected not to trust in chariots and horses (Ps. 20:7) but in the power and provision of the great *El Shaddai,* the Nourisher and Sustainer of His people.

"We will never again say 'Our gods' to what our own hands have made" (v. 3). In other words, the people's confidence was not to be placed in the work of their own hands. It is one thing to enjoy the things our hands have made; it is another thing to worship them.

The Act of Repentance

Repentance is a mind-set that looks to God for life, not resting on one's expertise, degrees, academic achievements, or business acumen. It does not mean that we cannot enjoy the fruits of our labors but we can recognize that life is not found in such accomplishments. "For to me, to live," said Paul, "is Christ" (Phil. 1:21). Not achievement, success, or the awards of applause of earth.

If in the act of drawing near to God we have within us only the elements of regret, remorse, reformation, or reparation, and if we are sorry only that we have lost our peace of mind and not the fact that we have misplaced our dependency, then we have not truly repented.

As we consider the act of repentance three obstacles may interfere.

1. Our failure to trust God's love.
Instead of basking in the security of His love, we so easily turn to other sources of life to deal with our personal pain. Whether other people or other substances, they are short-lived help.

2. Our failure to believe God's evaluation of our worth.
When our worth depends on other people's evaluation and estimation of us rather than God's, we move away from confidence in Him.

3. When we see no meaning or purpose in our lives.
We are beings with a destiny and with a purpose. God has a special purpose for every one of His children, and to refuse to see that is saying to God, "You are a Liar."

The Difference Between Cheap and Radical Repentance

Never be satisfied with cheap repentance which carries no power. Remember the root of sin is self-sufficiency—the ego in the place God has reserved for Himself. Cheap repentance is lopping off the branches rather than getting rid of the trunk.

True repentance requires real openness of heart and mind, a willingness to taste the absurdity of our sin, our false attempts at taking control, and our desire to remain intact without having to depend on God. We must come face-to-face with the fact that Jesus Christ is not an add-on—a turbo boost to an otherwise self-determined life but the center, for He really only fits at the center.

Jesus Christ is not an add-on, for He only really fits at the center.

Explain the difference between cheap repentance and radical repentance.

Cheap repentance is_____.

Radical repentance is_____.

Many individuals have come into the church but have never really experienced radical repentance. They are like the butterflies that lack color when there has not been much struggle as they have emerged from the chrysalis.

Let's consider one final truth. Repentance should not be an occasional thing in our lives. It ought to be regular. Whenever we feel ourselves moving away from dependency on Christ to lean on other things, we must recognize this pattern as misplaced dependency and repent of it. Regular self-assessment is needed. Repentance is a lifestyle. It is a positive thing. Don't see it as negative. It is turning toward something good on a regular if not daily basis.

A Case in Point

Repentance is a holy thing. It is the way we deal with our sins and with our wickedness. All serious communication with God begins in repentance. It is the door through which we come into the Christian life, and it is also the door through which we must pass whenever we find ourselves having moved out of relationship with Him.

The church at Ephesus was in trouble with the Lord because they had left their first love (see Rev. 2). They were commended by Christ because they were orthodox in their doctrine and efficient in their service. But in our Lord's eyes that was not enough. Christ chastised them because they had allowed their love for Him to lapse. "Remember the height from which you have fallen!" said the Savior to the Ephesian converts. Then He added: "Repent and do the things you did at first. If you do not repent, I will come to you and remove your lampstand from its place" (Rev. 2:5).

Why did the Savior encourage them to repent? Had they not done that at the time of their conversion? Of course. Repentance must be seen not only as the entrance into the Christian life but also the means by which we improve our Christian life. I have met many Christians who view repentance as a one-time experience, something to do at conversion and are never expected to do again. That is a fallacy. Repentance is continuous; it is the way we restore our personal relationship with God whenever we find that relationship has been disrupted.

The church at Ephesus, despite their spiritual industriousness, had moved away from a close and intimate relationship with the Lord. The only way back was through the door of repentance. We cannot hope to restore a close relationship with God unless we understand what it means to repent.

A Prayer of Repentance

Let me offer you a prayer of repentance. But before I do, let me tell you about Brunner's Law. The more a decision will affect your way of life, the more your sinful nature will enter into the debate. Other forces will militate against your saying this prayer and meaning it, not least of which is your own nature. How many times in your life have you attempted to meet your needs for security, self-worth, and significance outside of God? How God must feel as He sees you ignoring divine resources to make your life work? Ask the Holy Spirit to convict you of your need to repent.

Heavenly Father, forgive me for so foolishly trying to meet my needs in my own way when I know that You and You alone are to be my supply. I repent of my self-sufficiency and self-centerdness and ask Your forgiveness for my stubborn and arrogant refusal to trust You with my needs for security, significance, and self-worth. Help me Lord Jesus from now on to turn to You in daily dependency and draw from You, the uniquely sufficient God, all I need to hold my life together. In Christ's name. Amen.

Learning from the Mistakes of Others

Last week we left you with a question. What was King Saul's goal in behaving the way he did in the passage we studied? The answer lies in the following verse: " 'I was afraid of the people and so I gave in to them' " (1 Sam. 15:24).

Here we have it—clearly and precisely. His words reveal that he was more concerned about the approval of the people than the approval of God. He tried to meet his basic needs for security, self-worth, and significance in what the people thought about him rather than what God thought.

Saul was a people-pleaser. His goal was the commendation of the people. This explains his anger and resentment toward David, who at one time appeared to be more popular with the people than Saul. David was a perceived block to his goal.

Samuel saw through the fact that Saul's apparent repentance was nothing more than remorse. King Saul did not have a change of mind about where his life was found, which is real repentance. His life was not in God; it was in the people. He experienced no fundamental change of heart and mind.

Other parts of 1 Samuel show us that he did not understand what repentance is all about. He said in effect: "What I did was wrong but circumstances dictated it" (see 1 Sam. 13:11). "I have sinned but let me explain it" (see 1 Sam. 15:24). "I'd liked to have handled things better" (see 1 Sam. 26:21). There wasn't any evidence of a change of heart.

Saul struggled to get Samuel to come with him to face the people so that he might have prestige by association (1 Sam. 15:25). Samuel was greatly loved by the people, and Saul hoped the presence of the prophet would help him in his spiritual predicament. Again, however, Samuel saw through his subterfuge and told him that because of his disobedience and his failure to truly repent, the kingdom would be given to someone else.

Time seemed to be running out for Saul. Did he have time for repentance and a second chance?

Review the wrong approaches to repentance on page 83. Which one(s) most clearly reflect Saul's view of repentance?

The Death of Saul

Don't all of us prefer a happy ending? It would be great to find Saul at the end of his days as King having turned to the Lord and led his nation in a great spiritual revival.

Read 1 Samuel 31. How did Jonathan die? _____

How did Saul die?_____

The Israelites buried Saul with appropriate honor, but I wonder if they did so with many regrets. The king that they had asked for had died an ignoble death in battle, along with his heirs, having wasted his opportunities to go down in biblical history as one of the great kings of Israel.

A Diagnosis

In week 1, we asked you to give a tentative diagnosis of Saul. Now that we have surveyed all the areas of his functioning (relational, rational, emotional, volitional, and physical), we have the opportunity to sharpen and refine that initial diagnosis. We have also seen how the five keys to problems in the personality have worked their way out in Saul's life. What are your conclusions? Be prepared to discuss them at our week 7 session.

---

[1]Gerald Kennedy, *The Parables,* as cited in Selwyn Hughes, *Christ Empowered Living* (Nashville: Broadman & Holman, 2001), 203.

[2]Cornelius Plantinga, Jr., *A Breviary of Sin* (Grand Rapids: William B. Eerdmans, 1995), ix.

[3]Ibid., xiii.

[4]John White, as quoted in Hughes, *Christ Empowered Living,* 215.

[5]C. S. Lewis, as quoted in Hughes, *Christ Empowered Living,* 215.

[6]C. S. Lewis, *Mere Christianity* (New York: Simon & Schuster, Touchstone, 1980), 60.

Session 7: Making the Restoration Complete

∾

1. One of the reasons why Jesus Christ came was not just to save us from sin, but to enable us to _____ in the way God originally designed.

2. Attempting to change thinking, set the will in God's direction, and manage the emotions, without first understanding the need to repent of _____ _____ is in fact counter-productive and serves only to strengthen self-sufficiency.

What is it about the mind that needs reconstruction?

1. We need to understand the mind's core _____ _____.
   (The belief that we can be more fulfilled people by acting independently of God.)

2. We must continually _____ our minds to Scripture.
   (It tells us over and over again that without Christ we can do nothing.)

3. We need to learn to _____ on God's Holy Word.
   (It is not enough to read the Bible, study the Bible, or even memorize the Bible. Its power lies in inwardly digesting it.)

What is it about our wills that needs reconstruction?

1. What you do is what you _____ to do.
   (There are times in life when it may not feel like you have a choice, but always remember the loss of felt choice does not mean the loss of real choice.)

2. Behind most problems is an _____ _____ _____.
   (Once this is identified then it can be traced to a wrong belief, which will then necessitate a change of that wrong belief to a right belief.)

3. Make a _____ that determines every other _____.
   (The one over-arching choice that everyone needs to make in their lives—the choice that spells the difference between victory and defeat—is the choice to find our security, self-worth, and significance in God.)

What is it about our emotions that needs reconstruction?

1. Three suggestions for handling problem emotions:

   a. _____ them and _____ them.
   (You don't have to act on negative feelings, but they do need to be faced. Unacknowledged emotions cause trouble.)

   b. Discover how the emotion _____.
   (Problem emotions arise due to the frustration of a goal not being reached. Whenever debilitating emotions arise, seek to discover the possible goal that is being thwarted, what is hindering the goal being reached and what you might be telling yourself that is fuelling the pursuit of that goal.)

   c. Decide always to express negative emotions in _____ with biblical principles.
   (A Christian should never give free rein to negative emotions. Maturity means managing the feelings so that they are expressed appropriately and in ways that do not violate spiritual principles.)

2. A mature and growing Christian is someone who is aware of his or her

   _____, will seek to understand how they arose, and will seek

   to express them in ways that are in harmony with God's purposes.

MAKING THE RESTORATION COMPLETE

"Let us not become weary in doing good, for at the proper
time we will reap a harvest if we do not give up."

GALATIANS 6:9

Now that we have considered the important issues of the essence of sin and
the need for confession and repentance, we are ready to focus on how to
bring the three remaining sections of the personality—the mind, the will, and
the emotions—into agreement with the divine design.

Scripture makes clear that we cannot be at our best unless we are at our
best in Christ. We were made by Him and for Him, says Paul in his letter to
the Colossians, and it follows that we cannot function effectively without
Christ's leadership in our lives. "By him all things were created: things in
heaven and on earth, visible and invisible, whether thrones or powers or
rulers or authorities; all things were created by him and for him" (Col. 1:16).

Far from weakening personality, the indwelling Christ strengthens it.
The victorious life, the empowered life, is the life lived in Christ. When He
is at the center of our being—thinking, willing, and feeling in our responsive
hearts—then we begin to experience the kind of life God intended for us in
the beginning.

As you read, keep these questions in mind:
1. How do we allow Christ to be at the center of our thinking, our willing,
   and our feelings?
2. What are three critical issues in the restoration of our minds?
3. How can we responsibly express negative emotions?

We are in our seventh week of discovering what it means to experience Christ-empowered living. We have made the case that the damage caused to the human personality by reason of the fall is such that no reconstruction is possible through self-effort. Change must come from without. One reason Jesus Christ came was not just to save us from our sin but to enable us to function in the way God originally designed.

Every part of our personality needs to be touched by the power of Jesus Christ. Once we admit Him into our lives, then He lives within us to bring about the changes we need. In the last two sessions we explored (1) the relational aspect of our being and what it means to function there in accordance with the divine design and (2) the dynamic for change. In this session we are going to probe the rational, volitional, and emotional aspects of our being and how we can function according to the divine design in these areas of our personality.

Let me share with you one of the greatest mistakes I made in the early part of my ministry. In the first few years of my counseling experience, my focus in helping people with their personal problems was to try to get them to readjust their thinking, pursue the right goals, and manage their emotions. What I failed to understand for many years was that attempting to change thinking, set the will in God's direction, and manage the emotions was in fact counterproductive. Without first understanding the need to repent of misplaced dependency, my approach served only to strengthen self-sufficiency—the very thing that I should have avoided.

I now put a great emphasis on the fact that before a counselor sets about trying to help individuals think correctly, choose correctly, and manage their emotions, all this must be preceded by a sense of dependency on Christ. Otherwise, their counseling will be no different than secular counseling in which they are encouraged to do these things in their own strength. Never forget that "to live is Christ" (Phil. 1:21). When He stands at the helm directing our way, we can stay on course and experience the kind of life God intended for us in the beginning.

Believers point to Paul as an example of the life God intended for every Christian. Read Philippians 1:21; 3:7-8; 4:13 (margin). What empowered Paul's life?

_____

Rational

What do we need to understand in relation to the rational area of our beings? What is it about our minds that needs reconstruction? The Bible has a great deal to say about the mind. The words *mind, thoughts, think,* and *thinking* are found in Scripture more than three hundred times. God views the mind as an important part of human functioning. Today we will examine three critical actions needed to accomplish this restructuring. First, we need to understand the mind's core wrong belief.

Change must come from without.

"To me, to live is Christ and to die is gain."
—Philippians 1:21

"Whatever was to my profit I now consider loss for the sake of Christ. What is more, I consider everything a loss compared to the surpassing greatness of knowing Christ Jesus my Lord, for whose sake I have lost all things."
—Philippians 3:7-8

"I can do everything through him who gives me strength."
—Philippians 4:13

Three Critical Actions

1. Identify the core wrong belief.

Many thoughts go through our minds in the course of a day. One psychologist says that we think at the rate of 1300 words a minute. The big emphasis in secular and some forms of Christian counseling is on what is called *cognitive restructuring*, that is identifying those thoughts that cause us trouble, challenging them, and replacing them with different, more positive thoughts.

However, changing our thoughts without giving attention to the core wrong belief will not produce the radical change that the personality needs. Only with such change can spiritual health come to the soul. What is that core wrong belief? It is the erroneous belief that first plunged the human race into despair—the belief that we can be more fulfilled persons by acting independently of God.

Embedded like splintered glass in our minds is the foolish idea that we can find satisfaction for our souls through our own efforts. Satan is busy trying to keep that thought ever-present in our minds. Other thoughts that come into our minds also need to be identified and challenged, but this idea is where a change of thinking must begin.

> The core wrong belief is that we can be more fulfilled persons by acting independently of God.

2. We must continually expose our minds to the truths of Scripture.

Without Christ we can do nothing. Often we turn that text around and make it mean: without us Christ can do nothing. One of the ways I keep this thought always before me is to repeat to myself: "To me, to live is Christ" (Phil 1:21), then pause before repeating the word *Christ* and asking myself, *is Christ really my life or is my life found in something else?*

I have used this simple exercise with great effect in the counseling room. I would often say to a counselee at some appropriate point, "Finish this sentence for me: 'To me, to live is …' " Those familiar with Scripture would immediately say "Christ." Then I would say: "this time let's be absolutely open and honest. Are you saying that you draw your life wholly from Christ or from some other source?" More often than not that approach led to some deep heart searching as people realized that it is one thing to say that Christ is one's life; it is another thing to live in the reality of it.

Here are some of the answers I have heard in relation to this question when people have risen to new levels of openness and honesty: "To me, to live is control." "To me, to live is always being right." "To me, to live is getting my husband to pay attention to me." "To me, to live is constant approval." "To me, to live is money."

Have you arrived at this level of openness and honesty? Complete this sentence.

For me to live is _____.

> *"Don't let the world around you squeeze you into its own mould, but let God re-make you so that your whole attitude of mind is changed. Thus you will prove in practice that the will of God is good, acceptable to him and perfect."*
>
> —ROMANS 12:2, PHILLIPS

The church has within its ranks multiplied thousands of people who profess to find their life in Christ but who deep down find their life in something other than Him. The thought that Christ—and Christ alone—is our life must ever be kept in the forefront of our minds. Anything we can do to focus on that truth and remind ourselves of it is going to contribute greatly to our spiritual health.

3. Learn to meditate on God's Holy Word.

Bible meditation is a lost art in today's Christian society. Reading the Bible or even studying the Bible is not enough. The truths of the Bible become operational in our lives as we meditate on them. Thoughts can't just be fitted into the mind the way we put tapes in a tape deck. Because of sin, the mind resists. Such resistance must be overcome through patient and persistent application of God's Word to the mind through meditation.

Meditation is the art of taking Scripture and rolling it around in the mind until it becomes part of the spiritual digestive system. It means focusing on some part of the Bible—a word, a verse, or even a brief passage—until the Word becomes flesh in us. This may sound like work to some, but the life of God is not to be had on the cheap. It cost Christ a cross, and it will cost us something, too, in terms of time and effort if we are to experience health of soul. Wrong habits of thinking are not broken in a moment.

> The life of God is not to be had on the cheap.

Volitional

Once we establish in our minds the truth that life is found in Christ and not in other people or things, we are then free to pursue the right goals. The will is greatly influenced by the mind in the sense that whatever we believe will dictate the direction in which our will works. If I believe, for example, that money is the route to significance, then I will use every effort of my will to make money. There is nothing wrong in making money, of course, but that is not where life is found. If I believe erroneously that life is found in amassing a fortune, then all my efforts will be bent in that direction.

> *"Set your minds on things above, not on earthly things."*
> —Colossians 3:2

Our will follows our beliefs, and if in our minds we have a clear understanding that in Christ and in Christ alone real life is found, then our goals will be to know more of Him and to live according to His will.

When considering the subject of goals, keep in mind three facts.

1. What you do is what you choose to do.

Etch that into your thinking. You are always free to choose. In his book *Man's Search for Meaning* the well-known survivor of a Nazi concentration camp, Victor Frankl said, "Everything can be taken from a man but one thing: the last of the human freedoms—to choose one's attitude in any given set of circumstances, to choose one's own way."[1] We can choose how we respond to any situation, and therein lies our growth and happiness.

Maturity is recognizing that you can choose new goals, you can choose new behavior, and you can choose to view things from a divine perspective. Never say you didn't have a choice in a matter. Loss of felt choice does not mean the loss of real choice.

When you are asked about details of a church member's misfortune, do you have a choice in what you share? ❏ Yes ❏ No
What would you regard as spreading gossip?

_____

"Finally, brothers, whatever is true, whatever is noble, whatever is right, whatever is pure, whatever is lovely, whatever is admirable— if anything is excellent or praiseworthy—think about such things."
—Philippians 4:8

"We demolish arguments and every pretension that sets itself up against the knowledge of God, and we take captive every thought to make it obedient to Christ."
—2 Corinthians 10:5

Those with a hasty temper often argue that their personality is so wired that they have no choice but to respond to a negative situation in anger. Between the stimulus and the response, however, there is a moment, even though it may be a split second, when a choice can be made. The more we recognize that truth and decide to act upon it, the better our lives will be.

2. Behind most problems is an unrecognized wrong goal.
The major issue that brings people into counseling is that they are pursuing wrong goals based on wrong beliefs about what makes them feel secure, significant, and worthwhile. Once a wrong goal is identified, it is a simple matter to trace it to the wrong belief and encourage a change from the wrong belief to the right belief.

The wrong belief is the key because our goals follow our beliefs. When we try to change our behavior without changing the belief that supports it, great tension is produced in the personality. It produces strained Christians who do many of the right things behaviorally, but their thoughts are pulled in different directions.

Any attempt to give up wrong goals and strategies while believing they are the route to getting our basic needs met will be met with disappointment.

When you find yourself struggling with a personal problem that is serious enough to disable or depress you, remember this formula: behind most problems is an unrecognized wrong goal. Focus on what that goal might be, trace it to what wrong belief might be fueling it, repent of that wrong belief, and change it. You will find yourself getting back on course again.

Use this formula to analyze a problem that has caused you serious concern. Fill in the blanks. It only takes 30 days to form a new habit.

_____> _____> _____> _____
(Wrong Goal) (Wrong Belief) (Repentance) (Change)

Someone has likened the Christian life to the flight an airplane takes as it moves from one destination to another. It's amazing how a plane can take off from Singapore and land in London right on time. Take off at midnight and land at 6:48. How do they do that?

Before the plane takes off, the pilots have a clear flight plan. They know where they are going, but during the course of the flight, wind, rain, turbulence, air traffic, human error, and other factors act upon the plane causing slight deviations to the flight plan.

Barring extreme weather systems or the need to divert, planes usually arrive safely at their destination. The flight's safe and timely arrival depends on the pilots' constant feedback from control towers, other airplanes, and even the stars which enable them to maintain the flight plan.

In Scripture we have all the information we need to keep us on course. We have a clear flight plan and an accurate compass. Based on what we have been learning, it is possible for Christians to use these principles for counseling themselves. If Christians were to take the principles to heart and put them into practice, Christian counselors would have fewer issues to deal with. Don't take this to mean that you will never again need to call on the help of a counselor, but it does mean that many of life's problems can be resolved by applying these principles.

"The mind of sinful man is death, but the mind controlled by the Spirit is life and peace."
—ROMANS 8:6

3. Make a choice that determines every other choice.

Everyone needs to make one overarching choice that will spell victory or defeat in their lives—the choice to find our security, self-worth, and significance in God.

Consider for a moment one of God's great servants, the Apostle Paul. Without a doubt, Paul clearly understood that he was a goal-oriented being and that he had made a choice that determined every other choice. What was that choice? Second Corinthians 5:9-10 tells us: "So we make it our goal to please him, whether we are at home in the body or away from it. For we must all appear before the judgment seat of Christ, that each one may receive what is due him for the things done while in the body, whether good or bad."

Paul's one overarching goal in life was to please the Lord. This goal was based on Paul's belief that his relationship with Christ was the most important thing in his life. In pleasing Christ, Paul himself experienced fulfillment and joy. Just as Jesus pleased the Father (John 17), we too should make it our heart's desire to please God.

List some ways we can know we are pleasing God. If you need help answering this question, read Romans 8:28-29 and Galatians 5:16-26.

1. _____

2. _____

3. _____

Paul's goal could not be undermined or blocked, was never uncertain, and was fully reachable. In pursuing the goal to please the Lord, Paul had the guarantee of divine empowerment. God is always at work empowering those who seek to glorify His name in everything.

Consider what happens when we make it our goal—the one goal above all others—to please Christ in everything. When something happens that displeases you but your goal is to please the Lord, then you will consider His interests above your interests, and your actions and your behavior will follow a godly pattern. Even though you may be overlooked for a promotion, somebody may say something untrue about you, or someone may cheat and defraud you, if your goal is to please Christ, you will look to God for justice and not to man.

Emotions

If you make it your goal to please the Lord in everything, I promise that your life will never be the same again. Oh, you will be knocked off course, and you will be hurt and feel pain, but you will not be disabled or destroyed by your emotions because they will be tempered by the fact that you are seeking God's glory and not your own.

This leads us to consider that other important aspect of the personality—our emotions. How do we go about dealing with our emotions so that we are in charge of them and not the other way around?

We can take one of four ways to deal with our emotions. First, we can repress them—put them in deep freeze. Second, we can suppress them—be aware of them but keep the lid on them. Third, we can express them— blow up. Fourth, we can confess them—admit that we have them but keep them under control.

Number 1-4 your most usual way of dealing with emotions with 1 being most likely and 4 being less likely.

___ Repress   ___ Suppress   ___ Express   ___ Confess

No Christian can afford to go through life without clearly understanding how to deal with troublesome emotions. Let me remind you again that problem emotions are like the red light that appears on the dashboard of a car when something mechanical goes wrong. A modern vehicle has several computerized check systems built into it. If the oil level gets too low, for example, a red warning light will flash. The same happens if a door is not properly closed or if the brake and transmission fluids get too low. The red light alerts you that something needs to be done.

Something similar happens to us when our goals become blocked, uncertain, or unreachable. Problem emotions arise that signal some maintenance work is needed. We need to look at what is going on inside us.

Dealing with Problem Emotions

1. Face them and feel them.

When a troublesome emotion arises in the hearts of some Christians, they immediately look for a way not to feel it. That people will go to great lengths to deny their feelings has always amazed me. Christians are exceptionally adept at such denial. They read a text such as: "Everyone should be ... slow to become angry" (Jas. 1:19). So whenever they are angry, they pretend they are not.

You don't have to act on negative feelings, but you do need to face them and feel them. If you don't, they will drop back into your system and work counterproductively. Always remember that you never bury an emotion dead; it's always alive.

Frequently I find myself in the midst of people who are unwilling to face their feelings. Most often these are Bible-believing people, especially

You don't have to act on negative feelings but you do need to face them and feel them.

the more rigid brand, the same ones who are in love with the truth but afraid of the Spirit. Usually they are so fearful of being carried away by their emotions that they won't let even a little crack appear in the door. The consequence is nothing short of tragic—cold truth without the warmth of feelings.

Bereavement counselors know that people who do not grieve often become accident-prone because feelings leak out in one way or another. We should never attempt to block the awareness of an emotion. A quick prayer, a Bible verse—there is nothing wrong with these, of course. But they must never become a substitute for feeling the emotion. Emotions that are not faced and felt must be paid for later—in compound interest.

Unacknowledged emotions cause trouble. The more aware we are of our feelings, the sooner we can recover from them. Awareness is a key issue. You can't begin to deal with any problem emotion unless you first admit it is there.

The more aware we are of our feelings, the sooner we can recover from them.

2. Discover how the emotion arose.

How do emotions arise within us? They arise because a goal we are pursuing is either blocked, uncertain, or unreachable. So whenever one of the three dominant problem emotions arises in your life—anxiety and fear, guilt and shame, anger and resentment—and causes you a great deal of personal pain, ask yourself such questions as these:

- What is the possible goal that is being thwarted in my life?
- What is blocking that goal?
- What am I telling myself that is fuelling my pursuit of that goal?

Remember the formula again: If the dominant emotion is anger and resentment, then the block is something outside yourself—another person or circumstance. If the dominant emotion is anxiety and fear, then the goal is an uncertain one. It could be reachable, but you are afraid you might not attain it. You are probably depending on reaching the goal more than relying on Christ to make your life work. If the dominant emotion is guilt and shame, then you have set for yourself an unreachable goal. Because this goal is where you perceive life to be found, you beat yourself up with feelings of self-derogation. Self-inflicted guilt is often a device we use to browbeat ourselves.

Wise Christians understand that problem emotions tell them something about the goals they are pursuing, and they allow their emotions to alert them to the need for some fundamental changes in what they are pursuing.

3. Decide to consistently express negative emotions in harmony with biblical principles.

Christians should never give free reign to their negative feelings. Maturity means managing those feelings so that they are expressed appropriately and in ways that do not violate spiritual principles.

The mind and the will are meant to stand as censor over the emotions. We cannot choose whether a feeling arises in our hearts, but we can choose what we do with it. Feelings can be expressed in carnal ways or in godly ways. If someone has hurt you and you feel angry, then always remember that you can choose how you express the problem emotion. You can blow your top or, using the resources available to you through the Holy Spirit, you can pause to ask yourself: *Am I feeling this way because of some goal being blocked?* If the answer is yes, use the moment as a brief time of healthy introspection to see what is behind the negative response.

Trends come and go in the Christian church. Three or four decades ago there was a relational revolution in the USA in which groups met for honesty and openness sessions. They were a disaster. The idea was to be absolutely open and honest with each other in the interests of Christian growth and development.

So you would have conversations like this: "Betty, I must tell you that when I pick up the telephone and I hear your voice on the other end, my heart sinks. Your tiresome chatter and gossip bore me to death. In the interests of love I have to say that I have never liked you. Unless God puts love in my heart for you, then I doubt whether I ever want to speak to you again."

A man might say: "Bill, in the interests of openness and honesty, I have to tell you that I never want to play golf with you again. Your childish comments and reactions when you miss a putt make me feel like running a mile. I am glad to have gotten this off my chest, and I hope that you will now choose a different golf partner and leave me to get on with my life free from your childish ways."

What these people failed to understand was the principle that openness and honesty, without a commitment to another person's welfare, is not in the spirit of Jesus Christ. When we share with someone how they have upset us, that sharing must not be demeaning but controlled by a higher principle—love for others.

We must always express our emotions according to biblical principles of relating to others. Draw a line from the following Scriptures to the insights they provide.

Ephesians 4:29,31-32	Love others with God's love.
Philippians 4:8	Consistently do good.
James 4:17	Think worthy thoughts.
1 John 3:11	Speak with kindness and compassion.

Any emotion that interferes with our loving others as we are loved ought to be suspect.

Any emotion that interferes with our loving others as we are loved ought to be suspect. For example, that means we accept responsibility for the fact we are angry and say something like this: "I am feeling angry about this right now, and I want to deal with this in a way that glorifies Christ, but I do feel the need to share with you that what you said has caused me some inner hurt."

A mature and growing Christian is someone who will be aware of his or her emotions, seek to understand how they arose, and express them in ways that are in harmony with God's purposes.

Learning from the Mistakes of Others—

For the past six weeks we have been reviewing the life of the first king of Israel. We have sought to learn from his mistakes. Now we have come to the time of putting our knowledge together in order to discover how a man with so much to offer strayed so far from God's image.

A Diagnosis

Allow me to share my diagnosis of Saul, and you compare yours as you read. King Saul appears to be struggling with a deep sense of inferiority and inadequacy brought on by a failure to find his security, self-worth, and significance in God. He does not appear to have the inner resources for handling the challenges of life. He looks good on the outside but is troubled on the inside. Surely the more we study his life, the more clearly we can see that he considered the opinions of the people more important to him than God's opinion. Although he believed in God, he did not allow God to be sovereign in his life. As a result, he had little basis other than his own inner resources for dealing with the tasks before him.

Despite the fact that he had a strong physical exterior, he came across as spiritually bankrupt. He had a core belief that life could be found in the applause and admiration of others. As a foolish thinker, he had developed a wrong belief about where life was to be found. Perhaps the saddest comment of all is that he died by his own hand (see 1 Sam. 31).

As we look at King Saul, we see an image-bearer in whom the image of God had gone badly wrong. Let us remember that we are all on shaky foundations if our security, significance, and self-worth are not rooted in God. Keep in mind that although Saul was not consciously hostile toward God, he had relegated Him to irrelevance. Saul's problem was attempting to meet his basic needs in others rather than in God and shoring up his own ego. Let's make sure this is not our problem as well.

A Positive Case Study

One of the lessons we learn from a study of the Old Testament is that the character of a father is not necessarily the character of a son. At times that truth is unfortunate, as in the case of David and Absolam (see 2 Sam. 15–18). In the case of Saul and Jonathan, we can only wonder how Jonathan became such an admirable person. Certainly it was not the modeling of his father but rather an act of God's grace.

Read 1 Samuel 14. What clear instructions did Jonathan hear from God? Write your answer in the margin.

Relationally, Jonathan had an intimate relationship with God and with others. Jonathan was so certain of his communication with God that he was willing to stake his life and the life of his armor bearer on the message he would receive from God. His armor bearer did not just follow out of duty. He said, "I am with you heart and soul" (1 Sam. 14:7).

On another occasion, Jonathan would have been killed by his own father, but the Israelite soldiers stepped up on his behalf. "So the men rescued Jonathan, and he was not put to death" (1 Sam. 14:45). In 1 Samuel 23:16 Jonathan went to David at Horesh "and helped him find strength in God."

Perhaps you are familiar with the story of the friendship between Jonathan and David. After David's success killing Goliath, Saul became very jealous of David. Jonathan continued their friendship, risking his own life to save David's life (1 Sam. 20).

Rationally, Jonathan showed keen intelligence when he devised a plan to let David know whether it would be safe for him to remain in the immediate vicinity or whether it would be necessary for David to flee because of Jonathan's father's jealousy and temper (1 Sam. 20).

Emotionally, Jonathan was in touch with his feelings. He wept with David when it became apparent that they might not see each other again (1 Sam. 20:41). He possessed the characteristics of an enduring friendship—loyalty, trustworthiness, and affection.

Volitionally, Jonathan chose to befriend David, even though it could have cost him everything. Jonathan remained loyal to his father although Saul tried to kill him on more than one occasion.

Physically, Jonathan was a mighty warrior and won many battles for Israel. Although he was killed in the same battle as King Saul (1 Sam. 31:6), he had had an illustrous career as a protector of his nation.

I hope it has been obvious in this brief account of Jonathan's life that he had an intimate relationship with God which formed his opinions of himself and others. He found his security, self-worth, and significance in his relationship with God. He could have been called an image bearer, unlike his father, who was an image breaker.

A Mile in Their Shoes

Perhaps you have someone in mind, somebody who has always fascinated you and made you ask, "Why did God choose him or her?" Your challenge for our final session is to choose a Bible character to diagnose according to the five areas of functioning. Remember, however, to select someone who has a good deal of biographical information—enough material to analyze his or her behavior. Put yourself in his or her shoes.

If no one comes to mind, begin with the story of Jonah. Read the story several times. Ask yourself the following questions:

1. How does the character's relationship with God appear? Strong? Weak?
2. Do physical problems contribute to the issue?
3. Does he appear to be a person with the qualities of security, self-worth, and significance?
4. What appears to motivate the person? (Note: motivation is the urge or desire to get our basic needs met.)
5. Is a dominant problem emotion evident?

6. What do you consider the problem emotion to be? Guilt and shame, anxiety and fear, or anger and resentment?
7. What does this tell you about the person's most likely goal (undermined, uncertain, or unreachable)?
8. What do you surmise might be the possible goal?
9. What opportunities did the character have to repent?
10. How did he respond to these?
11. What could the character have done differently to avoid failing God?
12. In what way(s) am I like this person?
13. What do I need to do to avoid making the same mistakes?

Studying biblical characters and analyzing their lives from the five areas of functioning can protect us from repeating their folly as well as help us learn from their strengths. Use this same procedure on other Bible characters such as Gideon, Samson, Joshua, Elijiah, and so on.

Armed with the concept that everyone is an image-bearer, you need never wonder again why people do what they do. They pursue unbiblical goals and try to quench their thirst at leaky wells which in turn become their goals. When their goals are frustrated, the arousal of problem emotions incapacitates them and prevents them from living the abundant life that Jesus offers to all His followers (John 10:10).

Humbly record your observations. Let them inform you about how you intend to ensure that your security, self-worth, and significance are rooted in God.

---

[1]Viktor E. Frankl, *Man's Search for Meaning* (Boston: Beacon Press, 1962), 62.

Session 8: A Final Perspective

❧

1. In this final session we have one more aspect of the personality to consider—the physical. Scripture insists that we treat our bodies with _____.

2. Two opposite errors relating to the physical are that we _____ the physical altogether or give it too much _____.

3. Some Christians are more taken up with the care of their _____ than the care of their _____.

4. To treat one's body with disrespect is to disrespect God.

5. The irreducible minimum when it comes to physical health is to _____ right, _____, and maintain right _____.

6. The state of mind so affects the health of the body that whole categories of illness are now classified as _____ or partly _____.

A summary of the Christ-Empowered Living seminar:

- Sin is a declaration of independence.

- Because of sin, the image of God in mankind has been defaced and damaged.

- We desire to meet our needs for security, self-worth, and significance by asserting our independence rather than seeking to have them met in God.

- When Jesus came, the world witnessed for the first time someone whose personality fully reflected the image of God.

- Now Christ wants to take His place at the center of our lives so that He can empower us to live the life He designed for us.

- Christ alone can meet our deepest longings.

- He must have control of the center if He is to impart His power to us.

- Whatever we believe will meet our deep longings for security, self-worth, and significance will quickly become our goal.

- When we rely on something other than God to be our life, our goals can be easily thwarted and when they are, they cause emotions to arise, which in turn can become incapacitating and debilitating.

- Turning from self-dependency to God-dependency and relying on His love to give us security, His evaluation to give us worth, and His gifting in our lives to give us meaning and purpose is the secret of effective Christian living.

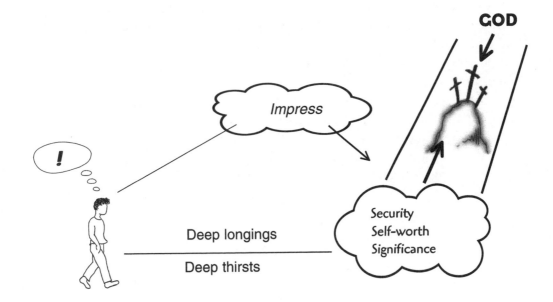

A FINAL PERSPECTIVE

❖

"Those God foreknew he also predestined to be
conformed to the likeness of his Son, that he
might be the firstborn among many brothers."

ROMANS 8:29

Grieg, the great Norwegian composer, was staying in a hotel in Oslo when in the next room he heard a woman practicing one of his compositions. He listened for a while, and being impressed with both the quality of her voice and her rendering of his work, he could contain himself no longer. Knocking on the door, he startled the woman who answered when he shouted, "That is how my songs should be sung!"[1] God did something of the same thing in relation to His Son when He was here upon earth. Three times He shouted from His cloudy pulpit as if to say, "That is how My life should be lived!"

Through the coming of Jesus Christ into this world and by way of His perfect personality, God revealed Himself anew to humankind. In the original Greek the word *conformed* is *summorphos,* which means *having the same form.* And what form is that? It is the form of Jesus Christ.

Just as the first Adam produced a son in his own likeness and after his image (Gen. 5:3), so the Last Adam, throughout this age of grace, is producing a progeny bearing a moral and spiritual resemblance to Himself. The fall marred God's image in man, and Jesus' purpose is to restore it.

Jesus is God's perfect man. Every fact of His wisdom reveals the wisdom of God's working in harmony with Him. Every manifestation of the love of His heart is the revelation of a mind given over to God, a heart that is fully in love with Him, and a will working under the constraint of eternal love.

Through Him Deity takes hold on humanity. Through Him humanity takes hold of Deity.

As you study, ask yourself these questions:
1. Do you treat your physical body with respect?
2. Which area deserves the most attention in your life: eating properly, exercising, or maintaining right attitudes?

In the final lesson of *Christ Empowered Living* we have one more aspect of the personality to consider—How can the physical body be restored to its maximum efficiency so that our relationships, thinking, emotions, and choices reflect empowered living rather than depleted resources? One thing is sure—Scripture commands us to treat our bodies with great respect.

Read Romans 12:1 in the margin. How are we to present our bodies to God? Underline your answer.

What do you think this teaching means?

_____

"I urge you, brothers, in view of God's mercy, to offer your bodies as living sacrifices, holy and pleasing to God—this is your spiritual act of worship."
—ROMANS 12:1

In 1 Thessalonians Paul says, "It is God's will that … each of you should learn to control his own body in a way that is holy and honorable" (4:3-4).

In week 4 (pp. 58-60) we were reminded that the body, soul, and spirit are connected. They affect each other so much that illnesses have been called psychosomatic. Although physical death is inevitable, we should strive to maintain the very best physical body possible for us. If we are sidelined in God's service due to mistreating the body, we have failed to glorify God with our choices and therefore limit our availability in His kingdom.

COMMON ERRORS

Christians can commit two equally opposite errors in relation to the physical aspect of their lives. One is to ignore the importance of the physical altogether, and the other is to give it too much importance. A balanced approach to the physical means we should care for our bodies but not pamper them. Some Christians are more taken up with the care of their bodies than with the care of their souls.

Give one example each of how we—

1. ignore our bodies: _____

2. pamper our bodies: _____

I came across this interesting translation of a verse from Proverbs which reads, "He who does not use his endeavors to heal himself is brother to him who commits suicide" (Prov. 18:9, AMP). To treat one's body with disrespect is to disrespect God. If the truth is faced, we treat our cars with more respect than our bodies.

A Christian medical doctor gave me some advice years ago that I have tried to follow. He said the irreducible minimum when it comes to physical health is to eat properly, exercise, and maintain the right attitudes. No doubt you have heard this advice from a variety of sources. Why is each of these essential? How do they work together to strengthen our bodies?

Eat Properly

A statement often heard in medical circles is that we dig our graves with our teeth. How true! Nutrition is so important. More than a millennium ago Hippocrates wrote, "Let your food be your medicine."

Dr. James McLester, a physician who lived during the middle of the last century, predicted that individuals who took advantage of the new knowledge of nutrition would be larger in stature, experience greater vigor, and live longer than their counterpoints. Certainly his predictions have come true. Eating the right foods is a necessary part of healthy living. Of course, the opposite is also true. Most of us, if we are truthful, know which foods contribute to poor health. Examine your reasons for the choices you make.

Exercise

Consider the issue of exercise. Our bodies were made to move, and we must keep them moving as much as possible. Don't be like the person I heard about who said, "Whenever I feel the need to exercise, I go lie down until it goes away." Many older people find their limb movements restricted because they have not exercised those muscles on a regular basis.

Right Attitudes

Our attitudes are as important as our arteries. Just as the physical can affect our moods, so our attitudes can affect the physical. There is a popular saying that goes like this: "You are what you eat." It could also be said that it's not just what you eat but what is eating you.

Dr. Stanley Jones, one of my mentors, "imagined a convention of bodies" meeting together "to discuss their inhabitants." He said:

> One body stands up and says: "I wish the man that occupies me knew how to live. He doesn't so I'm tied in knots half the time."

> Another body stands up and says: "The woman who inhabits me is afraid to live. She's always inventing ways to escape living. She drinks and smokes, hoping that will let her out. But each time I protest by a reaction into dullness and lethargy, she whips me up again. But it's all a losing game, and some day I'm going to quit protesting and I'm going to give up and die." It's too bad that these humans don't know how to live.

> Another body stands up and says: "Look at my condition. I'm all black and blue inside—and I'm showing it on the outside too. The person who lives in me has taken to be resentful toward life and has a chronic grouch. You should see how my gastric juices refuse to flow under these conditions. And now this silly person is dosing himself with medicines and running from doctor to doctor, who can't find a thing wrong with me. I know what is wrong: I don't work very well with resentments. I like good will."[2]

For more information about how to eat right, exercise and maintain healthy attitudes, go to *www.fit4.com* or look for the materials at *www.lifeway.com/fit4*.

Literalists might object to this dialogue and say our bodies do not talk. But they do—in the only language they know, the language of protest—and the protest shows itself through turmoil, disease, and pain.

As we said in week 4, medical people are now so fully convinced that the state of mind affects the health of the body that whole categories of illness are now classified as psychosomatic or partly psychosomatic. The disease is in the flesh, glands, or muscles, but it didn't enter the body by a germ or a virus; it came in by a thought, an anxiety, a diseased imagination, a conscience, distress, or a burning memory that has been unhealed perhaps. If disease can come in that way, then so can health. Divine healing is common in this sense; it happens every day. Christ-empowered living is also the healthiest way of living.

The road to ruin is often paved with good intentions. Like New Year's resolutions, good intentions will carry us only so far. Develop a personal wellness plan with both daily, weekly, and monthly goals. For more information on how to personalize your plan, order the *Fit 4 Accountability Journal* (0-6330-0589-4); 1-800-458-2772.

BACK TO THE GARDEN: THE ORIGIN OF SIN

Permit me now to summarize the problem, and then the divine solution, for mankind to reflect God's image marred by sin. Our first parents, Adam and Eve, though placed in a garden of exquisite beauty and perfection, failed to maintain their relationship with God by declaring independence from Him. That is what sin really is—a declaration of independence. Instead of depending on God and His Word and maintaining obedience to that Word, they chose to violate the divine command. By their sin they introduced into the universe the principle of pride which essentially says, "I don't want God telling me what to do."

When they sinned, the image of God that was in them became distorted and disrupted. They were like a broken lens reflecting broken light. They were still relational, rational, emotional, volitional, and physical beings, but they no longer functioned in the way they were designed. They could be described as magnificent ruins.

Adam and Eve's legacy, left to us as our sin nature, corrupted our personalities. Every part of our beings has been affected by the fall: our bodies, our minds, and our spirits. We still have longings for God. St. Augustine said that, we were made by God and for God and our hearts are restless until we relate to God.

Embedded like splintered glass in our souls is a desire to find our needs for security, significance, and self-worth in ways of our own making, thus asserting our independence. What is foreign to our fallen nature is the feeling of helplessness that must necessarily be there when we abandon ourselves to God in humble trust.

Have you ever prayed a prayer of desperation when you knew God was your best and only hope? Write what happened.

_____

_____

GOD'S DIVINE RESTORATION

We know that Christ came into this world, but the question that has to be answered is why? What reasons prompted the Trinity to devise such a humiliating plan? "For Jesus to become a man and live as a man amongst men," said the great preacher C. H. Spurgeon, "meant more humiliation than for an angel to become a worm."[3]

When Jesus came, the world witnessed for the first time someone whose personality fully reflected the image of God. In week 5 I suggested several ways in which Jesus completely met God's criteria for "image bearer." Let's briefly review those divine characteristics.

The Image of God in Christ

Whatever we mean by the elusive word *personality,* the least it could mean is that we can relate, think, feel, and choose. That is what constitutes the image of God in humankind. Nowhere did the image of God shine more clearly in human form than in the life and person of Jesus of Nazareth. In Hebrews 1:3 Christ is described as reflecting God's image.

Relational Image

Knowing the fullness of security, significance, and self-worth, our Lord's relationships functioned in the way they were originally designed. Over and over again we read statements like this: "The people thronged around him." "They could not get near to him because of the crowd." "The multitude followed him." Early in His ministry, except on those occasions when He withdrew to pray, He seemed always to be in the midst of a crowd.

Jesus related perfectly to rich tax collectors like Zaccheus; his personal friends Mary, Martha, and Lazarus; and the blind beggar. The Gospels are rich in incidents of Jesus befriending women such as Mary Magdalene. Whatever their status in society, Jesus was the great equalizer.

If Jesus were to walk on earth now with our generation, which places would you expect to find Him?

_____

In the margin, describe the types of people, races, and cultures that He might befriend today.

Rational Image

Rationally Jesus' mental capacity is manifest in the majesty of His dealing with all problems. In Him there was no clouding of intelligence. By reason of His sinless mind He saw all that was to be seen. Creation would have been an open book to Him. The ancient scrolls containing God's Word would have come alive with meaning and His communication with God would have been immediate and uninterrupted. These things can be said about no one other than Jesus. Our Lord was perfect in His mental makeup.

Volitional Image

In this analysis of Jesus' perfect personality, we must remind ourselves again of the interaction of mind, emotion, and will. Seeing God clearly and loving Him perfectly, Jesus gave Himself to God unreservedly. Our Lord's will was one with the will of His Father.

Jesus was always in tune with divine activity, always moving toward the goal of pleasing God. In Romans 15:3, Paul tells us "Christ did not please himself." Jesus' every movement and decision is a picture of a will yielded to the divine will. Even in His agony in the garden of Gethsemane, He prayed that God's will would be done.

" 'I seek not to please myself but him who sent me.' "
—JOHN 5:30

How do you seek to determine God's will in the big and small decisions you make daily? Check all that apply.

❑ Horoscope ❑ Friends' opinions
❑ Intentional prayer ❑ Church involvement
❑ Ouija board ❑ Christian books
❑ Bible study ❑ Tell God what you want

Emotional Image

Our Lord was no tight-lipped, unemotional ascetic. He rebuked hypocrites with burning but righteous anger—righteous because it was not a grudge at what was happening to Him but grief at what was happening to others. He looked upon a young ruler and loved him. The apostle John in his gospel called himself the disciple whom Jesus loved. Jesus' range of emotions, whether rejoicing in spirit or on occasion moved with compassion, reflects a multidimensional person with feelings in perfect control.

Match these Scriptures with characteristics of Jesus.

___ Matthew 9:10-13 a. Volitional
___ Luke 9:14-15 b. Relational
___ Luke 19:41-44 c. Emotional
___ John 4:34 d. Rational

Physically, Jesus' body took Him where He needed to go, traversing hills, mountains, and wilderness areas. If the body is the outer and visible sign of the inner and visible spirit, then the perfect spirit of Jesus expressed itself through a perfect physical frame. Disease was absent in Him. He had strength enough for the work of the day.

God spoke from His cloudy pulpit at the occasion of His Son's baptism: " 'This is my Son, whom I love; with him I am well pleased' " (2 Pet. 1:17).

Our Lord's coming into the world gave us a true picture of what God is like, reflecting His image to us.

On the line below put an X to reflect your answer to the question, How much does it mean to you to grow in Christlikeness?

|—————————————————————————————————|

Not a priority   Want to be Christlike   My heart's desire

The Christ-Empowered Life

In coming to this world, however, our Lord's concern was not just to reveal God but to reconcile us to Him through His death on the cross. Having paid the penalty for our sins on the cross, He made it possible for us to experience the forgiveness of sins and also Jesus Christ actually coming to live in every believer. Do you realize that Christianity is the only religion in the world whose founder came back from the dead to live in the life of His followers?

For two thousand years Jesus Christ has been coming into the lives of men and women and transforming them, rebuilding their personalities and helping them function in the way they were designed. It must be noted that Christ wants to rule our lives not as a president but as a king. A president serves for a period of time and then goes out of office. A king rules for life. It is one thing to have Christ in our lives; it is another thing to let Him reside permanently at the center of our being.

Many have professed to have welcomed Christ as King into their lives but then have sought to retain their own authority. Jesus Christ wants to take that place at the center of our lives and meet the deep longings of our hearts. He wants to be the one who meets our deep thirsts for security, significance, and self-worth. He is not willing to be shut out from even one part of our personalities.

Only as He has control of the center—that part of us where He belongs—can He empower us to live the life He designed for us. Surely this makes sense. If Jesus Christ is to empower us to live life the way it was meant to be lived, then He cannot consent to be excluded from any territory that Satan could use.

Pause now and ask God to show you any hidden areas in your heart that you have not released to Him.

> Christianity is the only religion in the world whose founder came back from the dead to live in the life of His followers.

Listen to Your Longings

The truth that God made us as longing beings has been strongly emphasized throughout this book. Deep in the heart of every one of us, we have been saying there are longings for relationship—first with the living God and then with other thinking, feeling, choosing beings like ourselves. Because we are made in the image of God, everyone reaches out to Him.

Understanding that we are longing beings and how to deal with those longings is crucial to keeping our lives on course spiritually. Permit me to lay down a few propositions to help you do that.

1. First, recognize your longings.

Fix in your mind that you have longings within you that nothing on earth can satisfy. Multitudes have said if they only had this or that, they would always be happy. Some have died believing it. The evidence shows, however, that when they obtained what they believed would bring them happiness, they found that it satisfied them for only a little while, and then the old persistent thirst came back, clamoring and demanding as ever.

2. Second, acknowledge your longing for God.

Only as you acknowledge your longings will you be able to move beyond them. Not to acknowledge unfulfilled longings is to be driven to search for satisfaction in other ways. One of the saddest things to behold is a Christian who remains content with practicing the duties of the Christian life—relying on them to bring satisfaction—rather than engaging in a dynamic and passionate relationship with God.

If we do not acknowledge our deep longings for God, we will remain satisfied with duty rather than devotion, with the things of Christ rather than with Christ Himself.

Our service for Him is important, but the most important issue in the Christian life is not what we do for Him but what He does for us. The deepest longings of our heart can only be met in a personal relationship with Jesus Christ.

If we do not acknowledge our deep longings for God, we will remain satisfied with duty rather than devotion, with the things of Christ rather than with Christ Himself.

3. Third, seek a passionate relationship with Him.

The only satisfying relationship with God is a passionate one. Several years ago, on the verge of retiring from active counseling, I sat down and began to think if a common denominator had been evident in the lives of the Christians who had sat in my counseling room asking for spiritual help. It did not take me long to conclude that one thing stood out above all others—lack of spiritual passion.

Many of these people were good Christians in many ways. They attended church, read their Bibles regularly, prayed, took care of their families, and saw themselves as dutiful Christians, but they appeared to have so little passion in their lives.

Some were ministers who saw themselves more as performers than desperately thirsty servants needing to drink daily from " 'the spring of living water' " (Jer. 2:13). I tell you again—with all the force and conviction of which I am capable—if we do not have a close and intimate relationship with God through His Son, Jesus Christ, no matter how dutiful we may be in observing the rules of Christian living, we will have little spiritual passion in our lives.

4. Tune in to your longings.

Tuning in to your longings means more than just acknowledging them. It means getting in touch with the fact that you are a thirsty, longing being. Focus on that fact and feel that thirst. Our desire to know God and enjoy Him depends on how aware we are of what we lack. The more deeply we feel our thirst, the more deeply we will drink of Christ and the more eagerly we will be drawn to the source of true satisfaction. So tune in to the deep thirsts and the deep longings within your soul. If you are not willing to feel the deep longings that God has placed within you for Himself, you will live on the surface of life and come to believe that anything can satisfy it.

Does this mean that when we learn to rely on God for security, significance, and self-worth that we no longer experience disappointment or need the love of others? No. We will still hurt, still be disappointed, and still desire the affection and affirmation of others; but if and when it is not there—providing our relationship with God is intact—we can still go on; we can still function.

People may hurt us and let us down, but they cannot destroy us. Our engagement with a living God does not insulate us from feelings of hurt or make us invulnerable to disappointment, but it does uphold us so that we can go on loving others as our own souls are loved.

5. Trust God to meet your deepest longings.

Turn from dependency on other things to dependence on God. *Trust* is another word for *faith*. Sin is antitrust. Many people in the Christian life can trust God with things like finance, healing, and choice of a career but are unable to trust Him with their longings.

Here's a challenge we must face. Can we trust God to meet the deepest longings of our hearts, the longings for security, self-worth, and significance, or do we turn to other things? To live a life of dependency on God means that we come before Him in absolute dependency, believing that if He doesn't come through for us, then we are sunk.

Take the following self-assessment to see if you listen to your longings. 1 = tone deaf and 5 = breaking the sound barrier.

I recognize my longings.	1	2	3	4	5
I acknowledge my longing for God.	1	2	3	4	5
I seek to have a passionate relationship with God.	1	2	3	4	5
I tune in to my longings.	1	2	3	4	5
I trust God to meet my deepest longings.	1	2	3	4	5

Is Christ Your Life?

Now let me turn in these final moments to talk to those of you who are Christians. Permit me to bring you back again to that famous text of the Apostle Paul, "for to me, to live is Christ" (Phil. 1:21). Is that statement true for you? Is Christ your life or is your life found in other things such as a career, money, music, performance, and so on? I am going to invite you now to put down your shovels and spades and give up every strenuous attempt to dig your own wells.

Commit yourself to Jesus Christ in a fresh way right now by determining to refrain from going down every false route to find security, self-worth, and significance. Develop a relationship with Him that will bring into your soul the aliveness that will prevent you from searching in other directions, one that will give you a goal that can never be blocked—the goal of pleasing Him in all things.

If you are ready and willing to do this, then join me in this prayer:

Heavenly Father, I see so clearly that I am made by You and for You. Nothing can satisfy my soul in the way You can. Forgive me for the wrong routes I have taken to find security, significance, and self-worth. In the future I want to look to You and You alone to be my supply. Help me from now on to make the great goal of my life to please You in everything I do. Show me even more clearly how to live in daily dependency on You, and whenever a pressing problem arises in my life help me quickly to get back on course. You provide the power, and I provide the willingness. I am willing. I close with this comment: right now and by Your grace and through prayer and the reading of Your Word, I intend to draw closer to You than ever before. In Jesus' name I ask this. Amen.

---

[1] Grieg, as cited in Selwyn Hughes, *Christ Empowered Living* (Nashville: Broadman & Holman, 2001), 162.
[2] Dr. E. Stanley Jones, as quoted in Hughes, *Christ Empowered Living*, 186.
[3] C. H. Spurgeon, as quoted in Hughes, *Christ Empowered Living*, 151.

Knowing Christ Personally

> *"Very rarely will anyone die for a righteous man, though for a good man someone might possibly dare to die. But God demonstrates his own love for us in this: While we were still sinners, Christ died for us."*
> —ROMANS 5:7-8

> *" 'Everyone who calls on the name of the Lord will be saved.' "*
> —ROMANS 10:13

> *"The wages of sin is death, but the gift of God is eternal life in Christ Jesus our Lord."*
> —ROMANS 6:23

> *"All have sinned and fall short of the glory of God."*
> —ROMANS 3:23

What are the steps we must take to have an intimate knowledge of God? Someone has described this decision as the master decision, one that shapes all other decisions down the line. It is the greatest and most important decision a person can make in this life.

God is eager and indeed longs to have a relationship with you, but He will never intrude where He is not welcome. Those who want Him must first decide that they really want Him—for keeps. He has made us free, and He respects the personality He has made.

Here, then, are the steps for knowing God:

First, consider carefully the implications of what is involved in entering into a relationship with God. The full title given to Jesus Christ in the Bible is the *Lord Jesus Christ.* The word *Lord* means that He is in full and total control of the universe. That is precisely the kind of control He wants to have in your life also. Look upon your commitment to God through Jesus Christ not merely as a surrender of your personality to His but as an unconditional surrender.

This decision does not mean you are expected to be a nonentity or a robot. It means that your life intermingles with His, your thoughts intermingle with His, and your will intermingles with His. But whenever your thoughts or your will clash with His, then His thinking and His will must prevail. This is the kind of commitment Christ asks of you. Do you consider this too hard or too demanding? There is a cost to becoming a follower of Jesus Christ, but the rewards are infinitely worth more than the cost. Think of what you get in return: forgiveness of your sins, God's life in yours, the certainty of His presence, help in every problem you face, and the guarantee of being with Him one day in heaven.

Once you are sure that you want God to come into your life, the **second** step is complete honesty and humility. One of the reasons we find it difficult to be humble is because of the perceived threat to our pride. The pride that is condemned in the Bible is the arrogant stance we take that puts the ego at the center of our lives instead of God. Nothing permanent can happen at the core of our beings until the ego capitulates to the claims of God.

The reason I say that the second step in coming to know God should be that of absolute honesty and humility is because I know from experience how this ugly self-centered being of ours will plead, excuse, and rationalize sin. It will allow marginal changes but will do its utmost to stay at the center. We can have no real encounter with God until we have the courage to face the sense of helplessness that comes when we realize we are being asked to give up self and have it replaced by God.

The **third** step in knowing God is a willingness to repent of the commitment to independence that lies deeply embedded in all our hearts. This desire to run our lives independently of God must be acknowledged before we can turn to dependence on God.

With a humble recognition of our need to repent, we must say, " 'There is no one righteous, not even one' " (Rom. 3:10). The **fourth** step is the acceptance of God's full and free forgiveness.

When Jesus was on earth, He forgave sins. Open your heart to receive His great gift of forgiveness. Allow no pride to hinder you. Don't pretend that you are better than you are. Look again at the cross. Christ died so that you might be forgiven. So go to Him now, and by faith take from Him the forgiveness of your sins with wonder and delight.

The **fifth** step on the road to knowing God is to trust God to be all that He has promised to be. Trust is really another word for faith. Basically, they mean the same thing. Some people think faith is peculiar to religion, but simple faith is found in almost every area of life. Whenever you board a bus, you exercise faith—faith that the driver knows his job. When you go to a restaurant for a meal, you exercise faith—faith that the food has been properly prepared and cooked.

No one can learn to swim without getting into the water. When all the movements have been explained and demonstrated, the time comes when one has to get into the water and trust oneself to its supporting power. If faith is everywhere, it should not surprise us to exercise faith in the process of getting to know God. In order to know God, you must turn from self-centeredness to putting all your trust in Him. Read what the Bible has to say about faith in Hebrews 11:6.

"Without faith it is impossible to please God, because anyone who comes to him must believe that he exists and that he rewards those who earnestly seek him."
—Hebrews 11:6

Scripture invites you to give yourself to Him now. You need no human intermediary to know God. Any man or woman can go directly to God through Jesus Christ. Think of Christ, the Revealer and Reconciler to God, as close to you now. Talk to Him now in your mind. This is what we call prayer—the mind reaching out to God.

If it helps, you might like to say the following prayer. If you decide to form your own prayer, then may I suggest you make sure it covers these elements: honesty, humility, repentance, acceptance of God's forgiveness, and simple trust. In this way I believe you will come to know God. Remember, we can only draw near to God in Jesus. If you are ready to pray this prayer, find a quiet spot where you will be uninterrupted; sit or kneel, and say these words sincerely from your heart.

" 'You will seek me and find me when you seek me with all your heart.' "
—Jeremiah 29:13

O God, I come to You now in the name of Your Son, Jesus Christ. I surrender my life entirely into Your hands. I make this choice, understanding the implications. Forgive me for keeping You out of my life for so long. Forgive my every sin. As I turn to You now in humility of heart, I receive that forgiveness according to Your promise and realize that I am free of sin through the sacrifice of Your Son on the cross. Help me to live a life that reflects Your love and power. Give me the courage to tell others that I have committed my life to You. I am now no longer my own. I belong to You. Thank You, Heavenly Father. I offer this prayer in the name of Jesus Christ, Your Son and my Savior. Amen.

 # LEADER GUIDE

This leader guide will help you facilitate eight group sessions for the study of *Christ Empowered Living: Reflecting God's Design*. Feel free to adapt the suggestions to fit the needs of your group and the length of your sessions.

Commit this study to God in prayer, asking Him to put together the people for the group He desires to participate. Continue praying throughout this study that God will use this time to do a mighty work in your church as your group members discover how to live a Christ-empowered life. Begin by enlisting the support of your pastor and church staff.

Getting Ready

Complete the following actions.

1. Begin publicity at least one month in advance of the first session. A promotional segment is included at the beginning of DVD 1. Show the 3-minute promo during Sunday School, worship services, and other church-wide gatherings. Display information about the course in high-traffic areas of your church facility.
2. Order a copy of *Christ Empowered Living: Reflecting God's Design* for each participant.
3. Make arrangements for a DVD/TV for the eight sessions. Reserve a meeting room that will allow each group member to see the TV well.
4. Sessions require a minimum of one hour.

Preparing to Lead

1. *Christ Empowered Living* is a video-driven course. Read "Meet the Presenter" on page 4 to become familiar with the video teacher, Selwyn Hughes, and his organization.
2. Read "How to Use This Resource" on page 5 to become familiar with the course model.
3. If possible, preview the eight sessions on the DVD before session 1 to help you as you lead discussions. You will know the questions that will be answered in later sessions. Also check out the bonus features on the DVD.
4. The lesson plan for each session lists the steps necessary to prepare for the session and gives suggestions for follow-up throughout the week.

Facilitating the Sessions:

Each lesson plan consists of five actions:

- Getting Started—Always begin on time. Share prayer requests and pray.
- Review—To encourage through-the-week learning and maximum benefit from the course, emphasize the importance of completing each week's study. This leader guide gives discussion questions and activities to be used during the session review. At this point, half of the session time should remain.
- Video Presentation—Generally 25 minutes.
- Viewer Guide—Participants will want immediate feedback on their responses to the Viewer Guide, so reserve adequate time following the video. Feedback will encourage participants' retention.
- Assignment—The week's assignment includes the reading material and personal learning activities that will reinforce Hughes' presentation. By calling attention to several of the activities, you will stimulate interest and encourage completion.

Group Size and Composition

- Since this is a video-driven course, your group can include more people than are generally enlisted for a small-group study. However, plan to enlist one facilitator for every 8-15 participants. The small-group facilitators would facilitate the first 20 minutes of sessions 2-8 while the large-group facilitator would be responsible for showing the DVD session, reviewing the Viewer Guide and the answers, and giving the next week's assignment. If you use this approach, refer to the lesson plan for session 8 for how to conclude this session.

Tips for a Successful Small-Group Experience:

1. The discussion questions given in each review section of the lesson plans are discussion-starters to be used as needed. Always begin by calling for members' questions, issues, and reflections from their study during the week.
2. Do not ask questions that are of a personal, private nature.
3. Focus on personal growth and not on agreement.

Session 1

Before the Session

1. Have copies of *Christ Empowered Living: Reflecting God's Design* ready for distribution.

2. Display the attendance sheet you duplicated from page 126 or prepare one for participants to sign their names, addresses, phone numbers, and e-mail addresses. Place this sheet on a table near the door along with pens, markers, name tags, and a basket for collecting money for books if appropriate.

3. Read pages 4-5, and be prepared to summarize the contents of page 5 during the session.

4. Provide a TV-DVD for your meeting place. Preview session 1 by selecting it from the main menu. Use the same procedure to begin the presentation of session 1.

5. On a markerboard or tear sheet, write the following statement.

> All behavior is caused,
> and the causes are multiple.
> —Selwyn Hughes

During the Session

1. As participants arrive, ask them to sign the attendance sheet, prepare name tags, and pick up copies of *Christ Empowered Living*. Invite them to leave payment for their books in the basket or offer another collection option.

2. Welcome the group. Ask for prayer requests and pray.

3. Introduce yourself and, depending on the familiarity of the group, give a little information about yourself. Ask members to do the same.

4. As a get-acquainted activity, form groups of 3-5 members. Direct attention to the author's statement on the markerboard or tear sheet. Announce that you will give each group a behavior to analyze and five minutes to find possible causes. Choose from the following behaviors, giving one or more to each group: daydreaming; unreasonable fears; compulsive worrying; teeth grinding; assuming the roles of the clown, the expert, or the flirt; always running late; chronic complainer; the bully; or the person who can't commit.

Give groups 3-5 minutes to report.

5. Ask the group to open their books and scan the table of contents. Then ask a volunteer to read aloud "Meet the Presenter" (p. 4). Summarize the information about using the study on page 5.

6. Encourage members to share why they chose to participate in this study and what they anticipate happening in their lives and in the life of your church as a result.

7. Instruct members to turn to the viewer guide for session 1 on pages 6-7. Ask them to fill in the blanks as they watch the DVD. Answers to the viewer guide blanks will appear on the screen underlined.

8. Select session 1 from the DVD's main menu.

9. Afterwards, ask one or more volunteers to read the completed viewer guide to the group. This step helps members retain what they have learned and clears up any confusion they may have about the correct response.

10. Then lead the group to discuss statements that were particularly meaningful to them or the decisions/actions they will take with them.

11. Invite members to turn to page 8. Ask someone to read the introduction to week 1. Read aloud the questions posed at the bottom of the page.

12. Assign week 1 in the member book for discussion at the next group session. Explain to participants that they will receive greater benefit if they spread their study over the week rather than attempting to complete all of it at one sitting. Encourage them to complete each learning activity for greater retention of the content they will read.

13. Read Revelation 4:11 from your Bible. Close with prayer. Ask God to give all members of the group open hearts to learn and grow as they commit to this study.

After the Session

1. During the week, call, write, or e-mail each attendee thanking him or her for participating in the study. Secure a commitment to continuing the study if the person did not make one at the first session.

2. Pray for yourself and for each person by name.

Session 2

Before the Session

1. Place the attendance sheet, name tags (optional), member books, pencils or pens, and Bibles near the door.
2. Provide a TV-DVD. Preview session 2 by selecting session 2 from the DVD main menu.
3. Write the four characteristics of God on four strips of construction paper. Mount each strip on one of the walls of your meeting room.
4. Secure a markerboard or tear sheets and markers for use in this session.

During the Session

1. Welcome members. Open with prayer.
2. Introduce the week's review by reading aloud the title for week 1. Brainstorm truths about God they have gained from this material. Write their responses on a markerboard or tear sheet. Encourage members to be specific with their responses and give examples.
3. Select volunteers to share how our knowing each of these truths about God helps us better understand ourselves.
4. Ask, *Do you think unbelievers need to hear and receive these truths about God? Why?*
5. Form four groups. Assign each group to stand beneath one of the strips mounted on each wall. Assign groups to explain how Adam and Eve reflected this aspect of God's character. After 2-3 minutes, ask for group reports.
6. Select a learning activity from each major heading of week 1 to review as a large group.
7. Introduce the section, "Learning from the Mistakes of Others." Read 1 Samuel 8:1-22. Ask, *What is a theocracy? Why would Israel rather have a king? What was Samuel's advice?* Explain that their assignment over the next five weeks is to come to some conclusions about how and why Saul defaced God's image.
8. Have members turn to the viewer guide and fill in the blanks as they watch the session 2 presentation. Then allow time for volunteers to read the completed viewer guide aloud.
9. Assign week 2 in the member book for the next group session discussion.
10. Ask anyone who prayed the prayer to receive Christ as Savior to meet with you after class.

(See p. 13.) Offer to help them with next steps in a new Christian's life. Close with prayer.

After the Session

1. Evaluate the session, asking:
   • Do members appear comfortable in the group?
   • Does everyone participate? If not, why not?
2. Contact any absentees before the next session.
3. Pray for yourself and for members by name.

Session 3

Before the Session

1. Place the attendance sheet, pencils or pens, and extra Bibles near the door.
2. Provide a TV-DVD. Select session 3 from the DVD main menu. Preview session 3.
3. Draw a friendly head of a snake on the top half of posterboard or a tear sheet. A smile and long eyelashes will help convey this attitude. Save room to attach clothing to your snake.
4. On another sheet of paper draw a pattern for a simple robe with long sleeves and no collar to provide the body for your snake. Reproduce multiple copies of this pattern. Bring markers and masking tape to the session.
5. Secure a markerboard or tear sheets and markers for use in this session.

During the Session

1. Welcome members. Open with prayer.
2. Introduce week 2's review by directing the group's attention to the first learning activity on page 23. Brainstorm descriptive words about the garden of Eden and what it was like living there. Record responses.
3. Ask a volunteer to state Hughes' conclusion to the question, "What was God testing by prohibiting the eating of the fruit of one specific tree?" (Would they obey or disobey?)
4. Then ask, *Do you think God knew the outcome of this test before He gave the order?* After several responses, assign someone to read 1 Peter 1:18-20. Summarize by saying that God was not caught unaware by Adam and Eve's sin.
5. Invite volunteers to share what would have been their reactions to the scene in the library (p. 23).
6. Discuss the ripple effect of sin, beginning with

the ripple effect of Adam and Eve's sin. Then ask, *What was the first sin?* (declaring independence from God)

7. Display the picture of the snake's head on a focal wall. Place masking tape beneath it. Remind members that the snake who appeared to Eve was a lovely creature, and today Satan comes disguised as attractive and alluring. Distribute the robes and markers until all have been given out. Instruct the group to label the garments with lures Satan uses today to entice us to sin. When finished, ask individuals to tape the robes to the bottom half of the poster.

8. Summarize by saying, *In a world that doesn't take sin seriously, we must proclaim the message that sin cost Adam and Eve and everyone who followed them everything. We have fallen from perfect reflections of God's image to broken lenses reflecting broken light.*

9. Form groups of 2-3 to practice review of Hughes' message in sessions 1-2 (see p. 27).

10. Refer to the section, "Learning from the Mistakes of Others." Review 1 Samuel 9-10. Ask, *What was Saul's reaction to Samuel's special treatment of him (9:21)? How did Samuel seek to encourage Saul (10:7)? What was Samuel's role in Saul's coronation? Why do you think Saul hid from his subjects? Which verse tells us there would be problems in Saul's reign from the start (10:27)?* Explain that we will add to this complex drama week by week.

11. Have members turn to the viewer guide and fill in the blanks as they watch the presentation of session 3. Then allow time for volunteers to read the completed viewer guide.

12. Assign week 3 in the member book for the next group session discussion.

After the Session

1. Evaluate the session, asking
   - Were you able to begin and end on time?
   - Were you able to complete each section of the lesson plan within the suggested time?
   - Do members need a reminder to arrive earlier? Do you need to end the session promptly at the agreed upon time?
2. Contact any absentees before the next session.
3. Pray for yourself and members by name.

Session 4

Before the Session

1. Place the attendance sheet, pencils or pens, and extra Bibles near the door.
2. Provide a TV-DVD. Select session 4 from the DVD main menu. Preview session 4.
3. Consult a Bible dictionary or study Bible for the meaning of *original sin*. Bring the reference to the session.
4. Bring to class a glass and a pitcher of water.
5. For this and the next session make a visual aid using a blank poster for background and 10 posterboard strips that you can attach one at a time with glue or tape. When finished, the visual will resemble this:

How Problems Arise in the Personality

Relational	Unsatisfied deep longings
Rational	Unnoticed wrong thinking
Volitional	Unrecognized wrong goals
Emotional	Unsettling negative emotions
Physical	Unsound physical functioning

During the Session

1. Welcome members. Open with prayer.
2. Introduce week 3's review by summarizing the introduction on page 36. Ask questions 1 and 2 at the bottom of the page, allowing for several responses. Inform the group that you will spend your review time dealing with question 3.
3. Focus the group's attention on the first learning activity on page 37. Ask, *What is original sin?* Write responses on a markerboard or tear sheet. Share what you learned from the resource(s) you consulted. Say, *Original sin means that we are born with a sin nature.* Ask, *What happens if we don't cultivate a relationship with God?*
4. Focus the group's attention on the symptoms of a thirst for God (p. 38). Ask members to share popcorn style what they wrote as you list them on the markerboard.
5. Display the glass and pitcher of water. Ask, *How full would this glass be if it represented our thirst for God?* Ask members to be honest in their assessments. Pour the amount of water the group agrees upon.

6. Read the statement in the margin of page 38. Invite responses to the question, "What other things do we seek to satisfy our souls?"

7. Then ask, *According to our author, what is the root cause of relationship problems? Explain your answer.* (fear, lack of trust)

8. Form three small groups, one each to represent security, self-worth, and significance. Ask each group to discuss and report on these issues: 1) define, 2) describe, and 3) give an example of both your key word and its opposite.
Call for groups to report after 3-5 minutes.

9. Lead the group to share their responses to the activities on pages 42, 43, and 45.

10. Display the poster of two aspects and two of the reasons why problems arise in the personality. (p. 46) Point out that other problems and reasons will be given in future sessions. Discuss the implications of these first two.

11. Refer to the section, "Learning from the Mistakes of Others" on page 46. Ask a volunteer to read 1 Samuel 13:1-15. Ask, *What was Saul's wrong thinking? What do we learn from Saul's example thus far in his reign as King?* Explain that in addition to Saul's volitional weakness, next week we will examine his emotional state.

12. Have members turn to the viewer guide and fill in the blanks as they watch the presentation of session 4. Then allow time for volunteers to read the completed viewer guide.

13. Assign week 4 in the member book for the next group session discussion.

14. Close with prayer.

After the Session
1. Evaluate the session, asking
   • Are you aware of any relationship problems facing any members of your group? Pray for them and for any specific leading if you are to be a part of the answer to this prayer.
   • Can you honestly say members are living lives of truth or folly?
2. Contact any absentees before the next session.
3. Pray for yourself and each person by name.

Session 5

Before the Session
1. Place the attendance sheet, pencils or pens, and extra Bibles near the door.
2. Provide a TV-DVD. Select session 5 from the DVD main menu and preview it.
3. From session 4 bring the visual for use in this session, including the poster, glue or tape, and posterboard strips.

During the Session
1. Welcome members. Open with prayer.
2. From session 4 review the relational and rational damage to our personalities as a result of the fall (first paragraph, p. 51). Display the poster listing these personality problems.
3. Review the definition of depravity from the Introduction to week 4 (p. 50). Ask volunteers to share their first memories of being disciplined for doing something wrong. Tell your story as a discussion starter. Point out that these stories happened while individuals were still very young.
4. Explain that secular humanists believe we are born morally pure. Any evil or corruption can be blamed on factors such as society, culture, parents, or the government. Lead the group to contrast the two worldviews and the implications of belief or non-belief in original sin.
5. Say, *We make a volitional choice when we live by a certain worldview.* Discuss the statements that (1) behind all behavior lies a choice, and (2) all behavior moves toward a goal.
6. Select volunteers to share answers to the activity at the top of page 53. Answers may vary.
7. Secure the strips on the poster containing the third aspect of the personality and its problem. Invite discussion to determine if participants understand the implications of this key to problem behavior.
8. Call for several responses to the activity on page 54. Emphasize the limitations of human willpower.
9. Turn the group's attention to the emotional damage caused by the fall. Ask, *What does our author say is the source of negative emotions? (p. 55) What goal did Adam and Eve fail to reach? What negative emotions did they feel?*

10. Form three groups, each representing one of the three main streams of problem emotions (p. 56). Ask each group to 1) name the emotions in their stream; 2) explain how their emotions relate to a failed goal; and 3) give an example. After a brief time for discussion, call for three-minute reports.

11. Attach the final strips to the poster. Discuss ways the body and the soul are intertwined. Encourage individuals to pay attention to the body's warning signals to avoid stress overload. Select someone to read aloud Mark 12:30-31 and Romans 12:1-2.

12. Review the negative example of King Saul from our study. Ask someone to read aloud 1 Samuel 20:25-31. Discuss these questions: What were Saul's dominant emotions? What were his blocked goals? What was his role model for his son, Jonathan?

13. Have members turn to the viewer guide and fill in the blanks as they watch the presentation of session 5. Then allow time for volunteers to read the completed viewer guide.

14. Assign week 5 in the member book for the next group session discussion.

15. Close with prayer for relational, rational, volitional, emotional, and physical healing so that we may serve God with our whole hearts, souls, minds, and strength.

After the Session

1. Evaluate the session, asking
   - Are participants completing weekly assignments? If not, why?
   - Since all behavior is chosen, what are they choosing instead?
2. Contact any absentees before the next session.
3. Pray for yourself and for members by name.

Session 6

Before the Session

1. Place the attendance sheet, pencils or pens, and extra Bibles near the door.
2. Provide a TV-DVD. Select session 6 from the DVD main menu and preview it.
3. On the markerboard or posterboard draw a winding upward trail with a beginning point, the trail, and an ending point. Label the beginning point, *justification;* the trail, *sanctification;* and the end, *glorification.* Be prepared to define these words. Consult a Bible reference if needed.

During the Session

1. Welcome members. Open with prayer.
2. Introduce the review of week 5 by asking, *If you were going to restore an antique table or classic car, how would you go about it?* List responses on the markerboard. Lead the group to arrange them in the order they should be accomplished. The list may include finding a replica or at least a very close model to follow. The model would inform you as to when you had reached your goal.
3. Make the point that when God chose to restore humanity to His image, He chose a replica of Himself. Ask someone to read John 10:30, 14:9-10.
4. Ask, *What does the finished product look like when God has completed His work of restoration in our lives?* Ask someone to read Colossians 1:27-28; 2:6; 1 Peter 2:21.
5. Say, *Becoming like Christ is a lifelong journey that doesn't end until death.* Display the drawing you made to illustrate justification, sanctification, and glorification. Entertain questions until you feel the group understands that restoring the five functions of the personality damaged by sin is part of the sanctification process that will continue until death.
6. Say, *This week we studied the relational restoration. According to our author, where do we find the best model for relating to others?* (the Trinity) Select volunteers to read John 16:7-15; 17:1-5,20-26.
7. Brainstorm types of relationships Christians often put before God. Write responses on the markerboard. In a sensitive manner allow a volunteer to tell an experience when he or she did not put God first in a relationship. Or, share an experience from your life. Summarize how God meets our deepest needs.
8. Select a volunteer to review the three steps in learning to pant after God (pp. 73-74). Emphasize that asking God for our needs is not the problem. The problem is asking amiss because we have not sought a relationship with Him that would align our hearts with His heart.

9. Review the King Saul story for this week from 1 Samuel 15. Read aloud verses 22-25. Ask, *Do you think Saul is truly repentent for what he did? What was Samuel's reaction? What might be Saul's goal in behaving the way he did in this chapter?*

10. Have members turn to the viewer guide and fill in the blanks as they watch the presentation of session 6. Then allow time for volunteers to read the completed viewer guide.

11. Assign week 6 in the member book for the next group session discussion.

12. Close with prayer.

After the Session

1. Consider offering a makeup session for persons who have missed one or more of the videos.

2. If viewing the missed sessions is not practical, offer attendees copies of the viewer guides with the answers filled in.

3. Pray for yourself and every member by name.

Session 7

Before the Session

1. Place the attendance sheet, pencils or pens, and extra Bibles near the door.

2. Provide a TV-DVD. Select session 7 from the DVD main menu and preview it.

During the Session

1. Welcome members. Open with prayer.

2. Select someone to review the opening story of week 6 about the compulsive sharpshooter (p. 78). Repeat the definition of sin as missing the mark. Ask, *Who is the only person who has not missed the mark?* (Jesus)

3. Recall Hughes' definition of the root of sin as declaring independence from God. Ask the group to play a game with you. Each person will say, "God help me . . ." followed by a sin, such as "God help me gossip." Continue around the circle until everyone has participated.

4. Draw the conclusion that we cannot be dependent on God and ask Him for help in wrongdoing. Independence—seeking freedom from God's control—is necessary to sin.

5. Point out that another aspect of sin is the I in the middle of the word *sin*. Challenge the group to think of a sin that has the good of another person as its motivation.

6. Summarize this discussion by asking these questions: *What is wrong with referring to sin as mistakes, blunders, bad timing, and so on? Is it helpful or hurtful to catagorize sin as big and little sins? Why is it essential for Christians to have a clear understanding of sin?*

7. Read each of the following statements and ask a volunteer to refute it (argue against it).
   a. We don't need to confess sins because God already knows them anyway.
   b. We don't need to confess ordinary sins.
   c. We don't need to get specific about our sins.

8. Discuss the issue of pride, which is a major obstacle to confession of sin. Challenge members to pray while on their knees as a symbol of a heart that is humbled before God.

9. Review the characteristics of false repentance by asking four volunteers to highlight the information from page 83. Then ask four other volunteers to change the false statements in the activities on page 84 into true statements of repentance.

10. Select volunteers who will share their definitions of cheap and radical repentance (p. 86).

11. Turn members attention to the character of Saul. Ask, *Did Saul need to repent? How was his repentance cheap repentance?* Then ask someone to summarize Saul's and Jonathan's deaths.

12. Remind the group of the assignment to offer a diagnosis of Saul at the next session. How and why did he deface God's image? Also assign the reading of session 7.

13. Have members turn to the viewer guide and fill in the blanks as they watch the presentation of session 7. Then allow time for volunteers to read the completed viewer guide.

14. Close with prayer.

After the Session

1. Begin thinking about an appropriate closure activity for session 8.

2. Ask your closed group leader or other church staff what study options will be available after this class ends. Be prepared to publicize them at session 8.

3. Continue to pray for yourself and the group.

Session 8

Before the Session

1. Place a gift for each person on a table near the door. Consider writing a personal note or purchasing an inexpensive message item such as a Christ symbol, a bookmark, refrigerator magnet, or greeting card.
2. Provide a TV-DVD. Select session 8 from the DVD main menu and preview it.
3. Make provision for any supplies needed for the closure activity that you have chosen.

During the Session

1. Congratulate members for finishing the study. Begin with prayer.
2. Call on someone to name the four parts of the personality that we have studied. Then ask another person to relate the problems that arise out of each part of the personality due to our fallen nature. (See poster from page 121.)
3. Summarize by saying that each of these must be brought into correspondence with the divine design in order to live the Christ-empowered life. Ask, *What is the key to victorious living?* (the life lived in Christ, Christ in the center, or in control)
4. Point out that Hughes' keen insight has alerted us to the sin of seeking independence from God. Because of depravity, we must regularly, as a lifestyle, confess this sin and repent of the desire to go our own way.
5. Lead a discussion based on pages 94-95, asking, *How do we allow Christ to be at the center of our thinking?*
6. Optional: If you have two who enjoy debating, assign the affirmative and the negative to this topic: What you do is what you choose to do. Allow five minutes and call time. Ask the others to express comments as well.
7. Invite a volunteer to share his or her response to the activity at the bottom of page 96. Or,

suggest the group think of a wrong goal based on a wrong belief and fill in the blanks together. Remind them that new habits are not hard to make if someone truly wants to change.

8. Summarize the healthy and unhealthy ways to express emotions. Review the scriptural ways to express emotions (p. 100).
9. Ask members to share in groups of three their diagnoses of Saul and compare and contrast them with the one on page 101.
10. Invite anyone who chose to prepare a case study of another Bible character to present it at this time. Thank them for their extra work.
11. Have members turn to the viewer guide and fill in the blanks as they watch the presentation of session 8. Then allow time for volunteers to read the completed viewer guide.
12. Be sensitive to anyone who may have had an emotional reaction to Hughes' words or prayers. Offer to meet with the individual(s) after the session.
13. Highly recommend studying the material for week 8 in the member book. Call attention to statements or activities that would interest your group.
14. Provide closure in the manner you chose before the session. Close with prayer.

After the Session

1. Often we ask God for guidance and forget to thank Him when He supplies our need. Spend some time writing answers to prayers you have prayed during the past eight weeks. Then, recount each one to God, praising Him for His provision and protection.
2. If there are still persons or situations that need your prayers, continue to be a faithful prayer warrior in the coming days.
3. Does someone in your church keep records of persons being trained in closed group classes? If so, report your group's attendance.

ATTENDANCE

Participant	1	2	3	4	5	6	7	8